What people are saying about *Life Without Pockets:*

"Carla's book brought me to tears as I learned how painful it was to need to hide her gender identity during the early chapters of her life. I laughed out loud at her hilarious self-deprecating sense of humor—unchanged by gender identity or the passage of time. I treasured her coming of age story from a 1950's privileged North Shore Chicago community which included a world immersed in the arts, creativity, friends and family. This is a lovely and practical 21st –century guide to living a life based not on the expectations of others, but on the continuing revelation and brave embrace of who we truly are."

—Marcy Smalley, author / City Planner, Kansas City, Missouri

"I must admit to bias, as I adore Carla and was bound to love this book. We have been lifelong friends since our first summer in this world. That was the summer our parents placed the two of us together in the soft caressing waters of our beautiful lake. Being only five months old at the time, I do not exactly recall that particular summer but all the summers since then have been filled to the brim with beautiful cherished memories. Reading 'Life without Pockets' was for me, both a fun experience and an awakening one. It was fun remembering the great people, wonderful old neighborhoods, and the extraordinary music of that time. Simultaneously I was awakening to the remarkable beauty and brilliance residing in the heart of my dear friend Carla. In these pages you are sure to find insight, laughter and perhaps a few tears; most importantly though, a view of the road less traveled."

—Janet Lee Downing, Waupaca, Wisconsin

"Drafting on a road bike involves letting the rider in front of you block the wind, creating an air pocket that virtually sucks you along, allowing you to ride faster than you can alone. And it's really fun. I've been drafting off of Carla's energy ever since I met her. Once you read Life Without Pockets, you'll understand why. Carla's book is informative, engaging, perceptive, and deeply honest. I was moved to laughter (frequently) and tears (occasionally). This is one journey everyone should read about. I'm proud of you, girlfriend, and I hope to be drafting in your wake for decades to come."

—Linda C. Grace, author / educator, Waco, Texas

"I've known Carla for a long time – in fact, my whole life – and her book reads just like how she talks. I can testify that it is authentic! But at the same time, I had no idea about the internal struggle she suffered through all those years. I'm glad she finally got her story told, and I hope others enjoy the book as much as I did."

—Tom Ernst, Denver, Colorado

"I read 'Life Without Pockets' in one sitting and found it to be compelling, informative, and an eloquent plea to humanity to get along, support each other and celebrate our differences. It's a wonderfully written account of a very personal journey and balances the pain and tribulations of rejection and intolerance – with kindness, support, and perseverance. Carla navigates through the highs and lows with élan, finesse and her trademark humor."

—Peter Lundberg, Director, Janus Galleries, Madison, Wisconsin

Life Without Pockets

My Long Journey into Womanhood

Life Without Pockets

My Long Journey into Womanhood

Carla Anne Ernst

HenschelHAUS Publishing, Inc.
Milwaukee, Wisconsin

Published by
HenschelHAUS Publishing, Inc.
2625 S. Greeley St. Suite 201
Milwaukee, WI 5207
www.henschelHAUSbooks.com

Please contact the publisher with requests for quantity discounts. We are happy to work with non-profit and academic organizations to help with building LGBTQ awareness and education.

ISBN: 978159598-551-4
E-ISBN: 978159598-552-1
Audio ISBN: 978159598-553-8
LCCN: 2017948154

Author photo: Meredith Watts

Printed in the United States of America.

Author's Note

A book autobiographical in nature touching on a shared child-hood experience could easily have been written by any of my six siblings (Barbara, Susan, Sally, Tom, George, or Elizabeth). But as my wise adult daughter Margaret said to me, "We all have our own truths." I recognize and respect that each of their stories would be different about the same childhood. Although I know that this is my story reflecting my memories, my assumptions, and my deepest feelings, I have also strived to obtain accuracy throughout the book. That being said, I hope you enjoy the book!

~ Carla Anne Ernst

Karis Anne Ross

Dedication

This book is dedicated to my friend Karis Anne Ross, who was with us until very recently when the pressures of constant torment, discrimination, belittlement, marginalization, and bullying caused this most beautiful soul to take her own life. Karis had apparently decided—after years of public advocacy toward extending civil rights and protections to transgender Americans, the steady stream of rejection she experienced in her personal and professional life resulting from her insistence to freely disclose her gender identity to all—were no longer worth the devastating sadness and feelings of self-loathing.

Words will never convey the loss that I—and so many others—felt of this tragic loss, a life taken way too soon, of such a sweet, kind, loving, and wonderful woman as our friend Karis. Karis was a beautiful and attractive woman—inside and out. I truly believe that her spirit is still with us—her grace and her charm, her kind little voice—now laughing and joking, telling stories of things yet to come, in a world that only she now knows. I loved her…we all loved her.

Hugs and kisses forever, Karis.

Also for Sarah Marie Ernst
and
Margaret Anne Ernst
who both inspire me to live an authentic life
with their unending love and support.
My love for you shall live forever

and

to all the amazing women and men who have
battled and endured through the darkest days.

Country road — photo taken by the author.

The Road Not Taken

Robert Frost

TWO roads diverged in a yellow wood,
And sorry I could not travel both
And be one traveler, long I stood
And looked down one as far as I could
To where it bent in the undergrowth;

Then took the other, as just as fair,
And having perhaps the better claim,
Because it was grassy and wanted wear;
Though as for that the passing there
Had worn them really about the same,

And both that morning equally lay
In leaves no step had trodden black.
Oh, I kept the first for another day!
Yet knowing how way leads on to way,
I doubted if I should ever come back.

I shall be telling this with a sigh
Somewhere ages and ages hence:
Two roads diverged in a wood, and I—
I took the one less traveled by,
And that has made all the difference.

Table of Contents

Foreword

Beautiful.

Carla Anne is beautiful. She is vibrant, articulate, candid, funny, empathic, and though she is loath to admit: extremely brave. She shares her life in ways few people ever do or will. She is heroic.

Life Without Pockets is beautiful. It reaffirms the importance of being utterly true to yourself despite the challenges, the fears, and the potential for rejection. Because the reader is allowed to experience, and more importantly, feel a personal journey of transformation, and of never-ending belief in the inner beauty of the self regardless of time or location along the gender continuum, this book is heroic.

And in a rather perplexing time when significant strides toward more complete acceptance of our fellow beings is met with equal resistance, *Life Without Pockets* is a harmoniously tuned voice reinforcing the need to remember that absolute beauty exists in all of us. Without labels. And in this case, without pockets.

But I am biased. I've known Carla since we were kids.

She was my very best friend. Actually, boyfriend I might add, but more importantly, my very first friend in Glencoe. Deep and long friendships go beyond gender or sexuality identity. We were pretty much inseparable. I followed his lead. I admired his imagination and creativity. I envied his energy. He was the brother I wished I'd had. Even my parents would ask—far too often for my liking —"Why can't you be more like him?"

But deep kid friendships can evolve over time. When differences in age and stage would dictate who played with whom. (Not to worry Carla: I won't mention you're much older than me—by one year). Changing family dynamics as well as a change in neighborhoods took me out of the picture and both of us out of each other's lives. For many years. Too many – far into adulthood. Although we didn't know it, we both gravitated to the same profession of marketing communications, nor did we know that we both ended up at senior levels at the same global marketing firm.

Cue the advent of social media, re-connection and reunion. This time with Carla. We picked-up exactly where we left off— though much had obviously evolved over that time. Same person. But in a more complete state of being. Same basic spirit. But with a greater sense of self and confidence. Same wonderful friendship. But with added dimensions of texture, nuance and finally – a real comfort in her own being.

These days I continue to admire her imagination and creativity. Her energy. And I feel she is like my penultimate big sister. A pretty cool transformation for both of us I reckon.

Truth be told: Carla has always been beautiful to me, and always will be. As is *Life Without Pockets*.

You should move on from the Foreword now and start reading the book itself. I'm willing to wager upon completion you too will simply say – *Beautiful*.

Peter Switzer, Dusseldorf, NRW

Preface

No single story about being transgender sums it all up. No one generally "chooses" this "lifestyle" as it's neither a choice nor a lifestyle any more than any other pre-designated category such as race, country of origin, disability, or ethnicity.

I did not anticipate writing this book. It started when someone once asked me if I had ever missed being a male. I thought about it for a while but couldn't think of anything significant I missed, apart perhaps from no longer having pockets. But then again, I'm kind of a "girly girl." Which to the amazement of my GG friends (genetic girls) who primarily dress androgynously anyway, and who sometimes ask why I wear such girly clothes, my answer is, "Because I can." At least I can now. That's the only big change I've come across so far in my gender "transition." And besides, who wants to wear all those boring guy clothes? My "coming out" is a very positive story, albeit spiked with a few challenges.

This story is painful to put into words. People have asked me many questions about what it's like to be transgender. Thus, this book is an "FAQ-styled" approach in response to those questions. Not just for my readers, but to some extent for me since I don't understand it all that well myself. Except to realize that being a woman seems right, comfortable, and normal to me. And to know that I'm fortunate to be able to live an authentic life. The typical questions that come to mind are:

- What is "transgender"?
- What's it like to be transgender?
- What's it like being transgender in a non-transgender world?
- What do I need to know to understand you? And,
- What do you want in your life?

This book started as a short email response to someone significant in my life who was struggling to understand and accept me. Someone who had consistently said to me that he "couldn't condone the choice I made" and that "I should get professional help." So, in an attempt to explain to him about the "choice" I had made, I realized my email needed broader context. Context to portray the world in which I grew up. The political, economic, cultural, social, theological, and religious mores, and the medical understanding of gender identity. But I never sent that email. Instead, the narrative ultimately evolved into this book. I think as much for my own sense of knowing, as well as communicating with the rest of the world.

As this book evolved, it went on a different path. It took on an unanticipated tone and purpose. It developed a life of its own—far different than the original misguided idea that a short email would diffuse the judgment and ostracism I experienced or lessen the pain and sadness I felt for so long due to hate and marginalization.

The shift in purpose came when I lost my dear friend Karis Anne Ross to suicide. Her death gave the book a definitive focus and intent. I have no desire to focus on negative energy. So now the goal of the book is simple. If it prevents the loss of just one life due to trans-marginalization or ostracism of any kind to any group of people, then in my view, the book has achieved its purpose.

Success to me is knowing my purpose. To grow to my maximum potential and be able to give to others who need it most. The book is designed to help others who have experienced what I have. And perhaps more importantly, to help others around them to understand—and possibly accept and support someone going through gender identity transition.

SECTION ONE

The World of Transgender

1. So, What is Transgender?

Transgender is a very broad term. The transgender community is diverse. It represents many labels, ages, perceptions, lifestyles, educational levels, races, religions, backgrounds, nationalities— and every other "group" or multiple groups into which people are. The word itself is evolving, and increasingly, is becoming better understood and accepted.

Some Background

It's difficult to get a precise definition of transgender as gender itself is complex and fluid. But a reasonably good one can be found from the American Psychological Association. The Association defines transgender, or "trans," as it is sometimes informally called, as an "umbrella term for individuals whose gender identity or gender expression does not conform to that typically associated with the sex to which they were assigned at birth and/or their anatomical development." It further states that "Gender refers to a person's internal sense of being male, female, or something else. Gender expression refers to the way a person communicates gender identity to others through behavior, clothing, hairstyles, voice or body characteristics."

Transgender people typically identify as female-to-male (FTM), or male-to-female (MTF). It's usually prudent to ask the person what he or she prefers regarding pronoun and name preference.

Transgender (not transgendered) can feel extremely disorienting, causing people to be desperate to align their body with whom and what they know they are. If they are unable to do this, they can be driven to extreme measures. Transgender people generally seek to live healthy, happy, authentic, and productive lives. Lives that reflect who and what they are, rather than face the relentless distress of trying to be someone or something they're not. Or what others may tell them they are or should be. To prevent pretending to be someone society says they are.

Self-identity has in part come to mean how individuals understand the way others perceive them, particularly with gender identity. Before the 20th century, a person's sex was usually determined entirely by the appearance of the genitalia at birth. But with the evolving knowledge about chromosomes and genetics, gender and sex are far better understood today.

Apart from the challenge of just being transgender, deciding to let others know is also extremely difficult, much like unveiling your sexual orientation—particularly not knowing how people will react. Some people need time to process the news and may never understand or accept the condition, while others can be accepting. There's a lot to take in, just as there's a lot to being transgender.

Unfortunately, transgender people live in a society that tells them that their deeply held identity is wrong or even deviant, leading to the loss of family, friends, employment, homes, healthcare, insurance, and other support systems. And worse, transgender people experience extreme levels of marginalization, harassment, violence, and sometimes death. Such experiences can be challenging for anyone, and for some people, can lead to anxiety disorders, depression, and other mental health conditions. These conditions are not usually caused in themselves by having a transgender identity, but instead, by the intolerance with which many transgender people have to experience. However, numerous transgender people—especially those who are accepted and valued in their communities—are increasingly able to live healthy, happy, productive, and fulfilling lives.

Sadly, the stigma associated with transgender identity has contributed to a precarious legal status, human rights violations, and barriers to appropriate care among transgender people. The U.S. psychiatric "bible" for diagnosing mental illness, the *Diagnostic and Statistical Manual of Mental Disorders, Fifth Edition* (DSM-5), recently reclassified transgender from "gender identity disorder" to a new state called "gender dysphoria." It states that it often manifests itself as an "intense feeling of pain, anguish, and anxiety due to the mis-assignment of sex at birth."

This revised diagnosis recognized that a mismatch between one's birth gender and identity changed from the idea of fixing a disorder, to resolving distress over the mismatch. Such a diagnosis contributes to viewing transgender people "as valuable members of society worthy of respect and human rights like everyone else." As a result, transgender is now viewed less as a medical condition since most transgender people don't experience severe anxiety or stress due to the difference between their gender identity and their gender of birth.

It's shown that easing of gender dysphoria occurs by expressing one's gender in a manner in which the person is comfortable. Today, major U.S. medical organizations recognize that living according to one's gender identity is an effective, safe, and medically necessary treatment for many people who have gender dysphoria.

Gender identity is not necessarily visible to others. When you're born, someone looks at your external genitals and automatically assigns you to a gender. However, that might not be how you feel inside. It is more about the internal sense of what and who you feel you are regarding being male or female, or somewhere in between, along a complex and shifting spectrum.

When people do align with the gender they feel inside; it's often called "transitioning." Although it varies significantly from person to person and has no set pattern, some people change their external presentation such as apparel, hair, and name. Some ask others to correct the pronouns used to identify them (e.g., "he," "she," "they," or even "ze," among others). Others use hormones or surgery to alter how they look and feel. Moreover, a constant source of confusion is that transgender people can be straight, gay, bisexual, or dozens of other conditions and identities. And to further confound understanding, gender identity has little to do with romantic attraction to other persons. For me, being transgender is not something I do just for the sake of doing it, for fun or sexual "high." It's much more about a profound sense of inner self and being.

Some of the common, related words that tend to get inter-changed and confused with transgender, but not the same, include:

- **Transvestite**—typically a straight, heterosexual male who sometimes wears and is comfortable in clothes traditionally associated with a female, and acts in a style or manner associated with a female. It's also called "cross-dressing." Cross-dressers can be confused with drag queens and drag kings. Generally, cross-dressers don't associate with the LGBTQ community and don't view themselves as being gay.

- **Drag Queen**—traditionally a male who dresses in female clothes or "drag," and often acts with exaggerated femininity in female gender roles and performing in highly entertaining drag shows. While usually associated primarily with gay men and gay culture, there are drag artists of all gender variations and sexualities.

- **Transsexual**—now considered an older term originating from the medical and psychological communities, the expression is usually brought under the broader terminology of "transgender."

- **Cisgender**—This is considered the opposite of being transgender. Often abbreviated to simply "cis," it is a term for people whose gender identity matches the sex assigned at birth.

- **Gender Fluid** – Also called "genderqueer," or "non-binary" (NB). This typically denotes a person who does not identify as having a fixed gender. It is a broad category for identities that are not exclusively masculine or feminine, thus outside of the gender binary. A gender-fluid person may also feel like a mix of the two traditional genders, rather than a person's sexual orientation.

- **Gender**, on the other hand, is an identity. It is something tied more to one's internal sense of being male, female, or somewhere in between, and social convention rather than biology. Where the confusion lies is that while for many people, "gender" and "sex" are correlated, they're not the same. There are many types, and manifestations of these notions now conveyed in growing lexis of terms, such as "androgynous" or "transfeminine" among others.

- Other definitions of transgender include people who belong to a **third gender**, a concept in which individuals are categorized—either by themselves or by society—as neither male or female. Societies such as North American indigenous cultures that recognize "Two Spirit" people, honor those with three or more genders among others.

- **Intersex**—This is a general term used for a variety of states in which a person is born with reproductive and/or sexual anatomy that doesn't fit the typical definitions of female or male. It often represents having a mix of both male and female reproductive organs. For example, a person might be born appearing to be male on the outside but may have mostly female-typical anatomy on the inside, or vice versa, or appear to be in between typical male and female types of genitals. A girl could have a noticeably large clitoris or lack a vaginal opening. Or, a boy could be born with a scrotum that is divided so that it has formed more like labia and/or a notably small penis.

Intersex anatomy may not appear until the person reaches puberty, finds himself an infertile adult, or dies of old age. Some people even live and die with intersex anatomy without anyone (including themselves) ever knowing. Formerly called hermaphrodites (historically and biblically often called "eunuchs"), intersex people are born with chromosomal and/or physiological anomalies.

The cause for intersex is a condition known as Congenital Adrenal Hyperplasia (CAH), or more commonly called *Ambiguous Genitalia*. Throughout the 20th century, doctors treated such intersex people at birth. They would use surgery to assign them one of the two most common sexes, usually to avoid stigmatization of the child or the family in the mind of society. This was a superficial solution since much of the patient's body may not be what the parent and surgeon chose. Today, that practice is slowly changing, in part because those kinds of surgeries are viewed as barbaric mutilation, and because many people no longer see being born intersex as a problem to be "solved." Further, our scientific understanding of who is and isn't intersex now goes far beyond structural matters of genitalia. (I happen to be intersex.)

Gender vs. Sexuality

Like all labels, nothing is black and white. There's plenty of gray area in between, and it's rapidly changing as gender is becoming better understood, recognized, and accepted as a part of society. One person might identify as transgender, another as a cross-dresser and not transvestite. As a friend who leads Columbia University's Institute for Research on Women, Gender, and

Sexuality once told me, "Gender identity is as complex and varied as the stars in the sky." Although gender is difficult to define, it's not difficult to know. Transgender is not a choice, disease, or sexual mode, nor an act of sex, lifestyle, or preference. It just is. As British historian, writer, and author Jan Morris writes in her book, *Conundrum*—it's a "passionate, lifelong, ineradicable conviction of who you are."

2. How Many People Are Transgender?

By the Numbers

Since many transgender people are closeted, no one knows the exact size of the transgender community, but as of this writing, the Williams Institute at UCLA School of Law has estimated that there are about 1.4 million adults who identify as transgender in the United States. Executive Director of the Institute for Transgender Economic Advancement Vanessa Sheridan puts the figure closer to 3.2 million people.

Among teenagers, diverse gender identities are more prevalent than people would expect. A survey went out to more than 80,000 Minnesota teenagers in 2016 that asked if they identify as transgender, gender queer, gender fluid, or being unsure about their gender identity. Approximately three percent answered yes to one or more—way more than previous research indicated. Published in the journal *Pediatrics*, the findings revealed that increasingly, U.S. teens are seeing gender as being more than just masculine or feminine. Youth are rejecting binary thinking and are asking adults to keep up. They don't always self-identify as the sex they were assigned at birth. Many reject the idea that "girl" and "boy" are the only options. This is likely due to a long history of advocacy, fighting for visibility, and more media attention on gender identity—that together—have increased visibility.

Dr. Daniel Shumer, a specialist in pediatric endocrinology, pediatrics, and transgender medicine at the University of Michigan, wrote in an accompanying opinion article in *Pediatrics*, that these higher numbers should serve as a message to schools and physicians to abandon limited views of gender. The American Academy of Pediatrics' policy now states that their members should incorporate gender-neutral words and encourage teens to feel comfortable when talking about their evolving gender and sexual identities.

3. Transitioning

(Note: Since I am a male-to-female (M2F) transgender woman versus a female-to-male (F2M) or "transman," much of this writing focuses on M2F, although most of the issues and concerns are the same for either "direction.")

Identity is complex. The transgender person comes to the realization—sometimes at an early age and sometimes later in life—that he never identified as being a male. A person once said to me, "Oh, you're just pretending to be a woman." What that individual did not understand is that if I was ever "pretending" to be someone, I once had pretended to be a male, at least early in my life.

People don't always decide to transition openly for various reasons. Maybe they're concerned about societal backlash, loss of friends, family, and jobs, the cost of medical treatments, or perhaps they merely think it indeed is no one else's business.

For many who realize they need to let the "woman" out in them or at least acknowledge her as being an essential part of who they are, it's often a very long and rough journey. They feel and usually know that they're female and recognize that they've always been so. Once they realize this, transwomen often start on a path of feminization.

This can include:

- Physical feminization, such as hormone regimens,

- Electrolysis and other types of hair removal

- Medical procedures such as sexual reassignment surgery (SRS), feminizing genioplasty, orchiectomy, or vaginoplasty

- Plastic surgery and chondrolaryngoplasty (also called a tracheal shave), to reduce the size of an Adam's apple

- Societal/ social changes, such as wearing feminine apparel and adopting a feminine lifestyle. Psychological transition through talk therapy and pharmacological treatment. Female hormones and testosterone blockers. However, even without any of these procedures, many still may identify as a female.

Note that transgender people may or may not choose to alter their bodies hormonally, physically, or surgically. But if they do, words that tend to be problematic are "sex change," "pre-operative," "post-operative," and "transsexual." The broader preferred term is usually just "transition."

4. A Binary World

Society speaks of binaries. Zero or one. Black or white. Good or evil. Blind or sighted. And of relevance here, male or female.

When we attempt to separate things into two neat (albeit artificial) "gender" boxes, this distinction may help society minimize their fears, but it does not reflect any scientific or medical thinking about gender identity. The populace tends to portray gender primarily from this binary perspective. However, gender is far more complicated to be represented in binary terms.

I've lived a life trying to fit into a binary world. In fact, this kind of thinking contributes to the problem, not the solution. In other words, this has led to the failure to differentiate between gender, sexual orientation, and anatomical body type. Trying to box transgender people into a binary system, when the universe itself is not binary, stigmatizes them for physical traits that are entirely benign. This kind of thinking causes us to ignore reality—something that should be an anathema to the rational thinker.

Gender scholarship indicates that "normative" societal thinking tends to get entrenched among organizations. This thinking becomes difficult to challenge, despite the supportive scientific evidence.

If we can look at society as a diverse group of individuals— even though heterosexuality might be the most common sexual orientation—albeit considered medically "normal," then we can more clearly see that human sexual orientation varies.

Some people happen to be straight. Some are gay, bisexual, asexual. And some a little bit of each. But this does not necessarily have to do with a person's gender identity or expression. In human cultures, sexual categories get pigeon-holed into male, female, and sometimes intersex, if only to simplify social interactions and maintain societal "norms." But reality and sexuality, like gender, are not measured solely by zeros and ones.

5. Gender, Sexuality, and Physical Anatomy

Society has little understanding of the three intertwined, yet separate, phenomena of gender, sexuality, and physical anatomy. Most people often intermingle these states of being. These three statuses are independent, yet interconnected, but are not the same thing. In general terms:

- **Gender**—Society typically associates gender with cultural behaviors such as dress, mannerisms, signs of deference, etc., but in and of itself, is not entirely a social construct that differentiates the sexes. Neuroscience research shows that gender is not the "one size fits all" mindset that's construed by society, but instead, has some inherent physiological and neurological characteristics that manifest, regardless of upbringing or environment.

  Gender is about identity and the inner sense of what and who individuals feel they are and identify as regarding being "male" or "female," or somewhere along that continuum since this is on a spectrum and can change over time. Today, scientists have characterized transgender as being more like stars in the sky—with everyone identifying in their own gender "space."

- **Sexual orientation**—The same as biological sex, this is the scientifically accurate expression of a person's innate physical, emotional, and romantic attraction to people of the same and/or opposite sex. This typically includes lesbian, gay, bisexual, and heterosexual orientations.

  Sexual orientation is usually (but not always) determined by characteristics of cell chromosomes or karyotype. It is about relationships with others and reproductive traits, defined by enduring emotional, romantic, sexual and/or affectional attraction to other people, resulting in a combination and spectrum of heterosexual, homosexual, bisexual, or asexual characteristics. This, too, is on a continuum, there's a lot of in-between, and it can change over time.

People are generally more familiar with the concept of sexual orientation, but much less so with transgender. And just like everyone else, transgender people have a sexual orientation, whether it be heterosexual, gay, lesbian, bisexual, or asexual. Note that some people can be offended by the idea of "sexual preference," which may suggest that if one is gay or lesbian, that it is a choice and thus "curable."

- **Body Type**— And thirdly, anatomical body type is about physical characteristics, genitalia, reproductive organs, and physical development. Bodies, of course, come in all different sizes and shapes. And biologically, many plants and animals can be both male and female at the same time, or at different points in their lives, such as in the family *Syngnathidae*, which includes seahorses, sea dragons, and other species.

6. LGBTQ Initialism

LGBTQ (or LGBTQI) is an umbrella initialism for persons who identify as Lesbian, Gay, Bisexual, Transgender, Queer, and/or Intersex. It is a self-designation that's been adopted by the majority of sexuality and gender identity-based community centers and the media. The initialism is intended to emphasize a diversity of sexuality and gender identity-based cultures. Its evolution is complex, controversial, and continually evolving. It began generally around the 1980s with LGB.

Used initially to replace the word "gay" when referring to the entire LGBT community, activists believed that "gay" did not accurately represent all those to whom it referred. Thus, LGBT evolved to emphasize a diversity of sexuality and gender identity-based cultures, often referring to anyone who is non-heterosexual or non-cisgender, instead of exclusively to people who are lesbian, gay, bisexual, or transgender.

The letter Q was added to recognize those who identify as queer—often conveying a political statement and/or sexual orientation. Q also advocates breaking binary thinking by seeing both sexual orientation and gender identity as potentially fluid. The term is a simple label to explain as best as possible, a complex set of sexual behaviors and desires. However, many older people feel the word queer has been hatefully used against them for too long and are reluctant to embrace it. Q can also stand for those who are questioning or in a state of flux with their gender and/or sexual identity.

The letter I was added to include intersex persons. This is also called DSD—Differences in Sexual Development. Thus, LGBTQI (or LGBTIQ) stands for Lesbian, Gay, Bisexual, Transgender, Queer, Questioning, and Intersex.

Some use LGBT+ to encompass a spectrum of sexuality and gender. Less common, the near-exhaustive version LGBPTTQQI-IAA+ evolved in an attempt to represent all the identities in the community. This initialism represents Lesbian, Gay, Bisexual, Pansexual, Transgender, Transsexual, Queer, Questioning, Intersex, Intergender, Asexual, and Ally.

Today, LGBTQ is a commonly used term initialism, possibly because it is more user friendly, easier to say and to remember. Perhaps down the road, all the initialism with dissolve when people are identified just as people.

7. Gender from Birth

Gender is complex. Studies show that transgender people have brains that correspond most closely to their gender identity, not their anatomical or physical body makeup.

Sexual differentiation starts to develop at about ten weeks in the womb. Trans people, too, become "wired" neurologically to be the gender they are. For example, a recent Boston University School of Medicine study review concluded that "there's a biological link to a person's gender identity, indicating that transgender people are essentially assigned genders at birth that don't necessarily match their inherent, physical, and biologically set identity." Thus gender "dissonance" can manifest itself very early on, often by age three, when children detect an incongruity between who they believe they are, how they're perceived, and what they're told they are.

Historically, children from birth are pushed by society into gender stereotypes—e.g., girls play with dolls, boys get trucks and footballs—all in a binary world of pink or blue. You certainly can see this cultural expectation when a baby is born, since the first question people usually ask is, "Is it a boy or girl?" This is further reinforced with stereotypical "boy" and "girl" notions, such as clothing, colors, toys, bathrooms, behaviors, and names ingrained throughout all aspects of society. For trans children, this pressure can be confusing and terrifying, often causing anxiety and from an early age.

8. *Oppression, Discrimination, and Violence*

Transgender people often face horrific abuse, discrimination, and violence. In the 2011 National Transgender Discrimination Survey Task Force Report, findings showed that transgender oppression remains pervasive throughout the entire spectrum of race, religion, age, culture, class, and economic conditions. Further, discrimination often leads to devastating outcomes.

Although transgender people are experiencing unprecedented media visibility, at the same time, they suffer from significantly higher levels of limited job opportunities, poverty, poor health, harassment, and isolation. In addition, they still face enormous barriers to their safety, health, and wellbeing.

Studies show that job loss due to transgender bias is at 55 percent, and more than 90 percent of transgender people are harassed, mistreated, or discriminated against on the job. Reported suicide rates among transgender persons is an astonishing 42 percent. This is not because transgender people are more unstable mentally, but rather, it is due to lack of understanding and acceptance. More than 57 percent of transgender persons experience family rejection. There is also violence. Some 64 percent are victims of sexual assault and many more of murder. In 2017, 28 transgender persons were killed in the United States, the most ever recorded. Some grim numbers.

The deeply ingrained beliefs that the characteristics of our physical anatomy mark us as a man or a woman—and that those are the only options—underlie much of the discrimination that transgender and other gender-nonconforming people face in our lives. These indignities account for the disturbingly high rates of unemployment, homelessness, and often suicide for transgender people.

For example, a recent notable suicide was that of a 17-year-old transgender woman in Ohio, Leelah Alcorn. Leelah threw herself in front of a moving tractor-trailer. She said in her note, "The only way I will rest in peace is if hate and mistreatment of transgender people stop. And that we become treated like human beings."

Hatred makes it challenging to live an authentic, happy, and productive life. As my story shows, the struggle resides in how friends, family, colleagues, and society treat us when we share this intensely personal detail about our lives. With negligible anti-discrimination protection, compounded by oppression, discrimination, violence, and sadly, suicide—these are the daily sobering realities for thousands of transgender people, in the world in which we live.

SECTION TWO

Being Transgender

"I felt trapped — not by my body,
but by a society that didn't want me to modify it."
—Juliet Jacques, journalist, critic, writer

1. I am a Woman

I currently live in Milwaukee, Wisconsin. I work as a corporate communications writer and consultant. I moved to Milwaukee from New York for the great weather. (It's minus 10 degrees today but should get up to zero by the afternoon. Wonderful!)

I'm adventurous and love the outdoors, such as scaling high mountains. But in Milwaukee, I can't find any to climb, so I've adapted to hiking up intersection curbs and walking on beautiful trails in the parks. I like to swim, kayak, race sailboats, and perform music. I play clarinet, flute, and saxophone (but not at a time) and am a composer. I love to go to parties, concerts, theater, ballet, museums, and off-the-beaten-path art exhibits. I also enjoy dining out, and like some women, love to shop 'til I drop.

Ethnically, I'm half German, half Irish, and a tad Scot—and I also have a little Scotch in me (just one pint). On a cold night, I'm happy to curl up by the fireplace and read a good book. Mostly history, theology, and philosophy (and a few ridiculous books in between), along with exceptional red wine and an excellent cheese (Wisconsin state laws dictate that one has to eat a lot of brats, beer, and cheese).

I'm also a transgender woman. This means that my assigned gender at birth doesn't match the gender I identify with today. For most of my life, I didn't understand what this meant nor could I articulate this in any coherent way. I also realized later in life that I have managed to suppress a great deal of this from the earlier part of my life.

Having been on a lifelong journey to womanhood—whether I consciously knew or understood it—I have no other gender to be. There was no other gender I could be. I only knew that I could not go on with my life trying to live in the wrong gender.

My experience, often like that of others like me, is about the challenge of trying to be someone you're not, while at the same time becoming who you are. And unfortunately, this war between my body and my gender, this dissonance or "dysphoria," can lead to painful situations, ranging from depression to suicidal ideation, job discrimination to societal marginalization. I have seen that happen to others—and to some extent myself—and now have had two friends take their own lives, one to whose memory this book is dedicated.

For a very long time now, I've lived and worked as a woman. From a mental, emotional, physical, spiritual, social, legal, and financial perspective, I am a woman. For this, I've also been taunted and harassed, and on at least two occasions, severely beaten, assaulted, and robbed.

For me, this has been an incremental and imperfect process. Most often transgender people have inklings very early on that their assigned gender feels out of sync with their bodies. This self-realization process is incredibly complex. You spend your life realizing that you're not who or what people say you are, so you start to hide your inner self. Then, at some point, as you become who you are, the reverse happens—you're forced to hide what you once were, or at least what people said you were. This is a strange phenomenon, but I'm way past the point in my life where I need to feel the need to hide anything.

Many years ago, I was compelled to have my external looks match my inner sense of identity. So, I transitioned at least on the outside to dress, act, speak and live as a woman to relieve the unbearable agony of incongruity I had lived for so long. Thus, when I first fully "transitioned" on the outside, I was finally able to communicate to and be perceived by others who I was inside.

Throughout this process, I sometimes collided head-on with societal transphobia.

This is humanity's panic in the face of uncertainty. It comes in the form of angst that many feel when confronted with the confusions, contradictions, messiness, non-precision, and multiplicity—when they can't immediately determine someone's background, disability, religion, race, class, identity, hybridity, mixed race, multi-ethnicity, transnationality, transculturality, or gender.

Gender identity is something they have little knowledge or understanding of as they search their databanks for gender-identifying clues. These clues would include expected behaviors, attire, voice, attitude, gait, facial expression, mannerism, vocabu-lary, body space, and presentation that overload if some detail doesn't come to the rescue in fixing the mysterious identity they can't grasp.

At the time of this writing, the United States was in the middle of a very divisive, nasty national political race. I don't know where it will all go, but Democratic presidential candidate Bernie Sanders' speech moved me which seems particularly relevant here in which he said:

> *"Our job is not to divide. Our job is to bring people together if we do not allow them to divide us up by race, by sexual orientation, by gender. By not allowing them to divide us up by whether or not we were born in America, or whether we are immigrants—when we stand together as white and black and Hispanic and gay and straight and woman and man. When we stand together and demand that this country works for all of us, rather than the few, we will transform America. And that is what this campaign is about. It's about bringing people together."*
> —Bernie Sanders, February 2016

Many transgender people contextualize their experience regarding a "transition." A reasonably effective word that describes a changing from one state or condition to another, or "journey" that many go through. But for me, throughout my entire life, whenever I looked into a mirror, I saw someone who I wasn't. I knew the person looking back at me was not who I was. I think the only "choice" on the table is whether or not individuals choose to live and work authentically as who they are—either privately or openly.

Thus, I find my journey is best characterized as more of a "realization" than a transition since I have always known who and what I was. This self-realization process is very complicated. Because of societal constraints, biases, prejudice, and marginalization, it's common for a person to try to avoid signs pointing to transgenderism, whether consciously or unconsciously. The mind does its best to help one survive, which can translate into triggering vehement denial, confusion, and sometimes profound shame and extreme pain.

People have asked me many questions, and I've always encouraged individuals not to be afraid to ask anything. I've also found that when I let people know the more intimate details about myself, it can sometimes give them a sense of comfort and allow them to share their understanding of sex, gender, and other identities. On the other hand, it also seems to give people "permission" to ask inappropriate questions, which I gathered at in the chapter "Don't Ask," and I have actually been asked.

My story is about the joys, pains, and sometimes horrifying distress that comes from my gender journey—by merely trying to live in the gender I am. For me, the story of my becoming a complete woman is more about a lifetime realization of uncovering the woman in me who was always there, rather than a transition.

"So, this changing sex thing. How does that work? Does it take a while or is it the sort of thing that might happen in the middle of a conversation?"
—Jeffery Russell, author

2. My Earliest Memories

People often ask me, "When did you first become a woman?" I like to say something like, "Tuesday, at noon. I went to my doctor and said I was tired of this 'man thing.' So she fixed it, I bought female clothes and went back to work."

The question is actually difficult to answer, since I have spent my whole life knowing I was a woman and becoming an all-embracing woman in one way or another. Although I may not have known what I was when I was quite young, I did know I was different. I buried my secret deep inside me telling not a single soul. However, I just didn't know what that meant or even how to articulate it until later in life.

Like most transgender women, I spent most of my childhood thinking about being a girl, secretly going through the cycle of wearing the clothing and then purging them, thinking this would pass (so to speak), not quite knowing that I was continually realizing my internal sense of true self, and intrinsically knowing that someday I could somehow simply be the person I knew I was. But I was reluctant, if not just outright fearful, to confide in anyone about my deep, dark secret. No matter how hard I tried, I couldn't be a boy. I couldn't be a real son, brother, or father. That's just not who I ever was.

I don't ever remember not knowing I was a woman. To avoid the double negative here, I should say I always remember being a woman inside—I did not "become" one. This is the gender identity I've always known as early as I can recall.

Suggesting that trans people "become" the gender they identify with can undermine the inherent nature of their identity, since it implies that their gender is something they chose at some point in their life. I know that non-transgender people have trouble grasping this concept, but my sense of "transition" is not so much about gender. For me, my sense of identifying as female has been the plumb line of my life.

Instead, meaningful transitions have been more about changes in understanding the importance of freedom, the inherent worth and dignity of every person, the maliciousness of prejudice and societal repression and fairness, and the import of compassion, respect, and acceptance.

Any significant change in me is more about having the courage to be honest and transparent about myself, being happy, deliberate, and whole, and about the revelation of the hidden human being who's been inside me my whole life. I've never had any significant gender identity "issues." I only had a gender identity just like everyone else. It's just that my identity was simply different than that of most other people.

Since I was born this way, it is all I ever knew. It was my own sense of being "normal" so I never had any internal conflict. At the same time, there were also times I felt that I didn't exist as a person, fearing someone would discover I was not actually a "real" male, let alone a "guy's guy," which is what society expected of me. I distinctly remember as a young child looking into a mirror and feeling that the image just wasn't me. I didn't know why, but it just wasn't me. Every day, I was reminded that my body did not match who I felt I was. It's a very strange and disorienting feeling.

I think I kept my gender identity a secret because I was terrified it would ruin the high expectations my parents, family, friends, and society had of me. They expected me to become a successful businessman. And I'm more than certain that those expectations did not include having me become a daughter, a sister, or businesswoman!

I also never understood why I felt this way. I just knew that I did. When I first suspected something was different about me and feeling like a female, I was in denial for years. This was a huge factor holding me back from discovering who I was. I grew up feeling like I'd never be able to be my true self. This made me feel sad—living a life that wasn't worth living. It's difficult to convey the internal distress it causes when every ounce of your inner being is telling you a truth about yourself that isn't matched by parts of your anatomy.

I continued to search for that authenticity of being my true self, but was forced to live a secret life. I lived in constant fear, felt utmost shame and guilt. I was desperately trying to maintain a cover in a society that still largely condemned (and still condemns) transgender people.

On one level, I wanted to get caught. Caught at being me. But I couldn't in society, at least not at that time. I was terrified. There was no one I could talk to. Growing up in a conservative, pre-Internet era and a stoic Catholic family—with virtually no communication or connection to anyone—certainly with no one like me. I had no information or context for what was going on in my body and mind, my sense of self, my sense of gender.

I even remember expressing my feelings several times with my wonderful pediatrician, the late Dr. Bennett Sherman, who was the only one who knew my even greater secret—I was born intersex—the amazing "kids' doctor of Glencoe," who then still did house calls with his black bag, but I didn't have the context or courage to talk about even though he certainly knew I was intersex. Besides, I was just happy he could fix my normal childhood ailments of bruised knees, colds, stomach aches, allergies, and other issues typical of any kid in those days.

In wanting to better understand my condition, at least physically, I recently spent about two years trying to track down my childhood pediatrician, Dr. Bennett "Buddy" Sherman. He was nowhere to be found. But after making numerous phone calls with undeterred diligence, I came across a nurse who knew where I might reach him. I called the number she gave me. A live service answered, and the voice tried to refer me to a pediatrician. I explained I was a bit old for a pediatrician, but that I was a former patient and friend of Dr. Sherman's. So, I asked the sensitive question as to whether or not he was still alive.

The voice hesitated, and said, "I am Dr. Sherman." Wow! I had reached him. Now 94 years old, he remembered me and my condition, and said he was not surprised I had become a woman. We talked for over an hour about many subjects, including transgender, and about his understanding and acceptance of transgender (he had worked later in his career with transgender children in Chicago). He also had a nephew who ran the transgender medical clinic at UCLA.

I told him about this book and he said he looked forward to reading it. I reminded him that once when I was young, he had asked me to repair a transistor radio of his, and I responded by saying I was too busy. He simply said, "Busy people get things done; that's why I asked you." Unfortunately, he passed away just as the book went to print. Well, Dr. Sherman, wherever you are now, I'm still busy, but I got this book done! (And the radio, too.)

Not until I was a bit older did I try to better understand and adjust to what society wanted me to look and act like. Unbearable fear kept me silent about my inner sense of self. But secrets can fester. They can viciously gnaw away at your inner psychological and even physical self.

I remember sometime after graduating from college in the early 1970s, reading about former tennis player Renee Richards' highly publicized Sexual Reassignment Surgery (SRS) and seeing her role as an early transgender community spokesperson. When I read the article, I thought, "Oh, my God! That's me!"

This remarkable relevance resonated with me and hit me very hard, with fears of the reality of what I might be as well, yet provided a small inner sense of hope that maybe I too could someday become the woman I knew I was.

Today, having lived as a woman most of my adult life, the idea of being transgender now becomes less relevant and more distant as I simply feel, live, act, and become a conventional woman. My sense of being a woman becomes no longer novel or unusual as I return to and connect with my inner self and let my soul guide me back into my life's pursuits.

3. My Early Days

In assembling a work about transition and realization that is autobiographical in nature, I think it's important to reflect upon where I came from, and to provide some context of the theological, social, economic, and cultural environment of the era in which I grew up. Perhaps importantly as well, to express the price of hiding—what it took to present myself to the world as a male, and how I protected my secret.

For the most part, I had a very happy childhood, at least on the outside, which gave me strength for an exigent life of transition and realization.

I was raised in suburban Chicago in the late 1950s and '60s. I am from a large, happy Catholic family, the oldest of seven children, reinforced by my extended family in the area, wonderful friends, and other families with similar values shaped by the community and mores of the times. I grew up primarily in the Village of Glencoe, a community perched upon the high bluffs of Lake Michigan in the heart of Chicago's upscale North Shore suburbs. Like many communities of the post-WWII era, the town provided a very traditional and conventional upbringing.

Glencoe then still had faint traces of being a former farm community, revealed by a few signs on the backs of old stores with peeling paint, revealing faded, sun-bleached ads extolling the products and services of a once-agrarian lifestyle.

The Village also had roots in part as a 19th-century summer resort community along the Lake Michigan shores for wealthy Chicago families, populated by a diverse amalgam of architectural styles—from Victorian "Painted Ladies," to Revivalist colonial and Tudor homes on sprawling green lots shaded by lush canopies of trees.

Many of the homes were designed by notable architects of the times, including David Adler, George Maher, Robert Seyfarth, Howard Van Doren Shaw, and later, Frank Lloyd

Wright and George Frederick Keck and brother William Keck, to name a few.

I had friends who lived in several of these elegant houses, and apart from the low ceilings and severe furniture, I did not have a full appreciation at the time of the architectural significance of the homes where I was delighting in after-school juice and cookies.

The ensuing village grew around what would become the Chicago & Northwestern Railway (C&NRR) in the 1880s, helping to make Glencoe a desirable place to live. This was reinforced by the construction of the Glencoe train station, still standing today, designed in 1891 by noted architect Charles Sumner Frost— designer of Chicago's Navy Pier, the C&NRR train station in Chicago (since demolished), and community train stations along

Glencoe Train Station

the way. I was lulled to sleep at night by the green and yellow C&NRR trains, dependably steaming through the town every hour like clockwork. (My grandfather once showed me his 1924 train schedule, which had not changed by one minute in all those years.)

The local grammar schools were each called North, South, and West, and the middle school in the center of town had an equally straightforward name—you guessed it—Central (my school).

Central School, circa 1940.

Glencoe also heralded a prestigious breed of notable citizens, such as Pulitzer Prize-winning poet, laureate, dramatist, Harvard professor, and Librarian of Congress Archibald MacLeish; film actors Bruce Dern (great-nephew of Archibald MacLeish),

Harold Ramis, and Lili Taylor; TV stars Fred and Ben Savage; author Scott Turow, author and former FCC Chairman Newton Minow; advertising legend Leo Burnett; and classmates of mine, including screenwriter Clayton Frohman, NIH Deputy Director Alan Krensky, parasitologist Frank Sherwin, photographer Jane Fulton Alt, economist and attorney Andrew Rosenfeld, and former Campbell Soup CEO Douglas Conant

Glencoe also has been the backdrop for many films, particularly by John Hughes. *Home Alone*, filmed next door in Winnetka, effectively captures the essence of much of the North Shore, as an amalgam of the sensibilities of the communities, values, and families, and to some extent, my own family. The exception was that my parents never left anyone home alone. At least not for long.

Once, however, while racing up to our summer cabin (not Paris) for vacation, my parents left my sister Susan at home. My dad realized this about 10 or 15 minutes out, and upon the discovery that one child was not in the nine-passenger station wagon, my mother was able to convince him that it would be prudent to go back for her. They did. They found her still using the facilities. They retrieved her, packed her up and we were on our way. Again.

As was true of many small towns of the era, we rode bikes everywhere. Doors were left unlocked. Crime was negligible. I regularly had overnights with friends and participated in numerous after-school projects. We often went to the Glencoe

Author holding up tree at Glencoe Beach. (Photo by Patricia Parcell)

Beach with family and friends and swam in and sailed on Lake Michigan.

On the Fourth of July, you saw tricycles trailing crepe paper streamers and heard their bells and horns, all to the strains of the school band playing Sousa marches for the town parade. In Glencoe's commercial district, or "Uptown" as it was called to differentiate it from Chicago, referred to as "Downtown," merchants knew your name. Credit was given simply by saying your name to the counter clerk. If you didn't have cash, they just put it on your account.

Uptown had changed little in appearance from the days when blacksmith and feed shops flourished, to today's modern upscale boutiques and specialty stores housed in many of the same buildings. In my day, though, there were certainly no chains, big boxes, luxury spas, or food boutiques. Mostly just practical goods. Many simply walked to market or drove a short distance to buy groceries.

There was one of everything, including the Glencoe Library, the Glencoe Bank (where my sister was a teller and "worked in finance," according to my boastful father). There was a gas station (where my two brothers worked pumping gas, or were "in oil" according to my father), the movie theater with 25-cent matinees, where I worked one summer as an usher. (And yes, I was in "pictures," according to my dad).

Another sister worked at the bakery supplying us with day-old baked goods until we overdosed on sugar highs. The gas station was staffed by real men in nicely pressed uniforms with

Glencoe Movie Theater, ca 1946

shiny name tags and matching caps, always ready to enthusiastically pump gas into our fathers' station wagons at 25 cents a gallon while they checked the oil and washed the windows.

There also was the Barber Shop, which had Pete, the venerable, red-nosed, stoic (and slightly hungover) barber/jazz clarinetist who provided the obligatory buzzcut of the era for 25 cents, and for me, free advice on jazz improvisation. There were no restaurants, but Glencoe did have two great delicatessens—Ricky's and Miller's—always stock full of lox and bagels, gefilte fish, kreplach soup, and other tasty delicacies.

Weineke's Hardware Store, with its wonderful wooden floors, tin ceilings, and old-fashioned cash registers was a long-time fixture of Glencoe's business district. It carried everything from kitchen pots to toy tops. To me, it was a vast museum of wonderment, providing ongoing exploration of science, art, and astonishing electrical gadgets.

There also was the ever-popular Ray's Sport Shop, jam packed with the latest sports merchandise. It was run by the eponymous Ray, the "coach" of the enterprise, with slicked-back black hair and a Salvador Dalí-like mustache, always attired year-round in short-sleeved summer shirts and a whistle around his neck, selling only the high-priced brands.

By far, the all-time best hangout was Wally King's Record Shop, run by Wally King and his wife Diane, a former 1940s big-band drummer and singer, respectively, who together owned the amazing store that sold actual records—45s that delivered the weekly new Beatles hit song, and later LPs, heralded as providing the newly-invented, mind-blowing "stereo-phonic sound!" way before CDs and MP3s. How much better could hi-fi get!?

Everyone one knew Ray and Wally, and they knew everyone else.

Glencoe also had a sizable Jewish population. There were two synagogues, one of which was the notable North Shore Congregational Israel with its soaring sanctuary on a 19-acre Lake Michigan bluff. It was designed by the prominent Japanese-American modernist architect Minoru Yamasaki, best known for the original World Trade Center. Most of my friends were Jewish, both male and female. I seemed to connect with their rich culture. On Jewish holidays, my Jewish friends were dismissed from school, and we remaining kids were herded into a single classroom. On several occasions, I attended temple class with my friends—to the point that I just assumed I was Jewish, too.

I sometimes spotted the numbers on the arms of some of my friend's grandparents, revealing that they were Holocaust survivors. Although nowhere near the horror of what these people had experienced, I did, however, connect with them through my own private sense of ostracism, living constantly in fear, hiding my dark, inner secret.

There wasn't a Catholic church in our town, so we were schlepped to one in the next town to go to Mass.

This was also an era steeped in intolerance and marginalization. I speak from what I know. From what I experienced firsthand, whether from a comment muttered under a breath or outright bigotry.

I certainly didn't yet know that transgender people were a marginalized group in society, or that there even was such thing as a transgender person. However, they were victims then of anti-LGBTQ violence and hate crimes. These were rarely reported. And those that were, were not investigated. Transgender people lived in hiding, with discrimination and injustice at every turn. They were tortured. They were mutilated. They were killed.

This was hardly part of my life. I had assumed I would conform to the expectations of the community and follow the well-traveled road to predictable monetary and societal achievement like everyone else. This was how I was raised and all I knew.

Although I tried to conform living in a gender that wasn't me, at the same time, I would look into the faces of family and friends, yearning to be like them. To be "normal." So why was I saddled with this horrible burden? It left me feeling isolated and lonely inside. Terrified that my thoughts and feelings would somehow be discovered.

With the mores and values of my community, I innately knew that if I had ever conveyed my inner feelings to family or friends, it would be unlikely that I would be understood or accepted. The consequences would have been severe. So, deep inside, I continued to harbor my gnawing secret that only continued to deepen and fester – a secret not shareable with anyone. Who could I confide in? Where could I turn?

This was horrific for a child to live with day in and day out, hiding my secret. So, one succumbs to living a double life, trying to be part of it as much one can, and yet always hiding on the inside.

Today, Glencoe is an affluent and well-educated community. I write this rather detailed chapter about the town I grew up in—not to profile it, but rather to provide the context of my upbringing and its impact on my internal struggle with gender identity. I paid a high emotional price for hiding—trying to present myself to the world as a male while fiercely protecting my secret.

Regardless of the disparity between who I was inside and the male I presented myself as, Glencoe remains an important source of reference and serenity for me.

As the first child, I naturally received a lot of attention from my extended family, at least for a brief time. But then our family grew and my sole-child status was relegated to becoming just one of seven kids—first just me, then three sisters.

Life Without Pockets

Sally, Sue, Barb (and me)

Then Tom (in my lap)

Then two more, the twins. George & Elizabeth

4. My Parents and Grandparents

When my parents married after World War II in the late 1940s, it was then considered to be a "mixed" marriage between a Catholic woman and Lutheran-born man.

Roger & Ann Marie Ernst wedding

Although my parent's wedding ceremony apparently took place in my grandparent's backyard, for historical accuracy, their wedding license says they were married "in St. Athanasius Parish" (Evanston, Illinois). I don't know if that's intended to portray the parish as a geographical area that included her parents' backyard, or if it's supposed to mean they were married in the parish, meaning the church. Regardless, the ceremony took place in my mother's parents' backyard in Evanston, Illinois.

My mother, Ann Marie Ernst, was somewhat shy and introverted, but very kind and visually talented. My dad, Roger Wesley Ernst, was a fairly intense, mercurial, and hard-working businessman. He was also extremely witty and had an innate sense of musical sensibilities. Although never trained, he would often pluck out melodies on the piano with one finger to Chicago's then light jazz station WSDM ("Smack Dab in the Middle") with its all-female DJs. Another time, once, and only once, I heard him sing a solo at a scout campout around the campfire, astonishing everyone with his tenor voice singing, *Oh, Danny Boy*.

In 1886, Chicago was the printing capital of the country when Omar Merganthaler, the German inventor of the Linotype machine, set up shop in what became known as Printers Row. Although the publishers and printers are long gone today, one can still decipher trace remnants of these businesses through the old buildings, some with their original signage, touting their original publishing house names. Today, Printers' Row comprises many of the old buildings converted into upscale residential lofts. Today they boast the prestige of living in the coveted Printers' Row neighborhood with their narrow blocks and wide windows providing maximum sunlight that illuminates books hidden in the ornamentation of early Chicago School Architecture terra cotta murals, depicting the history of the printing press.

My father and his father, Louie Ernst, went into the printing business and started Ernst Printing Company, initially in

Printers' Row. They later moved it to 560 West Lake Street, then in the heart of a grim row of stolid, brick manufacturing buildings in Chicago's West Loop.

When I was young, my dad's printing plant also was the destination for my birthday parties—clearly the birthday party of all parties for all my friends at the time. Hey, what could be more fun than letting dozens of pointy-headed little kids run around a printing plant with giant rolls of paper, hide in large boxes, play with piles of type and cans of ink inherent to a printing plant?

This was topped off from back in the days when cholesterol was just another unpronounceable word with a lunch at a real Chicago steakhouse nearby, the memorable and now long-gone Barney's Market Club, a national shrine noted for its steaks, serious drinks, and its "Yes, sir, Senator!" slogan.

Inside, you were engulfed by its deep-grained, dark-wood paneling and ceiling fans illuminated by rows of porcelain wall and ceiling light fixtures tracing the pilasters. In its heyday, it was a mecca for many disreputable and somewhat shady characters, including politicians and sports teams from the nearby Chicago Stadium. Of course, this experience was hard to beat in terms of feeling like real grown-ups. Where else could a 10-year-old boy be called "Sir?" (Although I would have preferred to hear, "Yes, Ma'am, Senator!")

Today, the area has long since been cleaned up, gentrified, and beautified, and has evolved into the hip Near-West Loop Neighborhood, boasting all the standard upscale affectations of coffee bars, fitness clubs, juice bars, and moms with fancy baby strollers.

My father was extremely outgoing, personable, friendly, very funny, and a lot of fun. For example, I remember a time once as a young parent when I was home alone taking care of my then-toddler daughter Margaret after she had just swallowed a dime. I went into a complete panic. (I didn't know then that infants swallow all sorts of things and usually survive.) Regardless, I grabbed her feet, erroneously thinking I could easily dump out the dime like a marble stuck in a Coke bottle. I ran to the phone with my upside-down daughter in hand to call 9-1-1. But as I reached for the phone, it rang and it was my father (who rarely, or more accurately, never called me). I exclaimed (more like screamed) that I couldn't talk right then since my young daughter had just swallowed a dime.

There was a pause on the phone. He then said, "Don't worry. I can lend you a dime."

What a relief! In those days, a dime was a lot of money. And "lend?" I think what I'll always remember most about this trauma is that he said "lend" me a dime. That was my father.

Thrifty and frugal. Funny and fun. German. A tough-love kind of guy. Of course, swallowed dimes—at least just one—generally don't kill children. Apart from requiring some significant washing, dimes generally make it through the digestive system unscathed.

Having completed a tour of duty as a WWII Navy fighter pilot, he always claimed to have, "won the Big One by finishing up the Pacific Theater." (However, I think he spent most of his time transporting cargo planes in central Oklahoma, perhaps less heroic than he may have conveyed.)

My father's passion was aviation, which continued throughout his life. We were the beneficiaries of this when we were young, as he would take us up in a Piper Cub—a small, simple, lightweight, training plane known as the "Model T" of airplanes

Roger W. Ernst

at what was then Sky Harbor Airport in Northbrook, Illinois. He also took us out to the then-recently built Chicago airport, O'Hare, to see planes take off and land all day (how fun!). My dad's passion continued throughout his life as he enjoyed the Experimental Aircraft Association (EAA) air show in Oshkosh, Wisconsin, much later in his life.

My father came from a middle-class, German-American Protestant family. This was reflected in some level of their austerity and strictness, Christmas kitsch. It also brought with it great German potato salads, homemade apple pies, lima bean casseroles (actually made with ever-so-yummy butter beans, with a recipe handed down to my cousin Kathy Geertz-Schopp and shared with me!).

Dad grew up in Edison Park, a far-northwest section of Chicago (but still "da City," as any native Chicagoan would tell you). This was further confirmed to be a great place by Dan Quale, who said, "It's wonderful to be here in the great State of Chicago." But for me, I knew that gender identity certainly would not be a subject that could ever be broached in that type of environment.

My dad's parents were my grandfather, Louis "Louie" Wesley Ernst (Dec. 9, 1896–Mar. 15, 1975), and my grandmother, Laura Flossie (Korbmacher) Ernst (Aug. 4, 1899–Aug. 21, 1981). I learned a great deal about my paternal family from our family genealogist and historian, my cousin John Geertz-Larson, the son of my dad's older sister, Lois (Ernst) Geertz.

Louis Ernst, circa 1975

Grandpa Louie was kind of a jocular man, essentially a crusty mix of Spencer Tracy and Jimmy Durante. He worked mostly as a printer, and at some point, as a welder building O'Hare Airport, confirmed by his pronouncement, "Who would ever build an airport in the middle of nowhere that no one would ever use?" (He would not have made a great visionary.)

Always with dozens of rubber bands on his wrist due to his profession as a printer (I guess assuring people that he was always prepared to bind up a loose pad of errant papers)—at Christmas Eve family gatherings, my grandfather would play along with his *Dukes of Dixieland* records on his cornet. He also had a soft spot for us kids. He encouraged us young "musicians" in Christmas carols. Essentially, we were a ragtag group of young musicians in our early forays of learning the tuba, trombone, piccolo, violin, accordion, drums, and other assorted instruments that together made the Salvation Army street-corner bands sound like finely tuned symphonic orchestras.

Grandpa Louie was born in Seattle, Washington, the youngest of twelve children, seven of whom survived past early childhood. (Interestingly, I am one of seven children and my dad's brother, Donald Ernst, also had seven children.) Louie may have been named after his uncle, Christian Ludwig Ernst, who had changed his name to Louis C. Ernst when he came to America. Louie's older siblings were all born on their parents' farm in rural Richardson County in the southeast corner of Nebraska.

Louis Ernst as an infant in a dress on his father's lap

Louie's father was Adolph Ernst, who had been born in a small southwestern German town Spöck in the Upper Rhine River valley near the Black Forest. In 1868, Adolph was brought to America by his parents at the age of 14. Louie's mother was Pauline, who had been born to German immigrants in Buffalo, New York. In the mid-1860s, Pauline's family moved to St. Joseph, Missouri, just across the river from Richardson County, Nebraska.

Adolph and Pauline met and married (likely in the Missouri/ Nebraska region). By this time, railroads had begun replacing the stagecoaches, wagon trains, and steamboat river crossings from St. Joseph that had previously fueled the area's economy. Adolph and Pauline, along with most of their families, later moved to the Seattle area, which was rebuilding and growing following the Great Seattle Fire of 1889.

Adolph owned a Seattle grocery store with one of his nephews, and also worked as a carpenter.

In 1883, two of Adolph's brothers, Charles J. Ernst and Fred Ernst, opened Ernst Hardware in downtown Seattle. The store grew into a major regional chain of home improvement centers, Ernst Home Centers, Inc. By 1994, at the company's peak, the chain operated 95 stores in 12 western U.S. states. In 1997, though, the chain filed for bankruptcy and was liquidated.

In July 1899, Adolph and his sister Magdalena (Helene), still living in Seattle, joined the Christian Catholic Apostolic Church of Zion (CCAC), a forerunner of the Pentecostal movement founded by faith healer (and con artist) John Alexander Dowie of

Chicago (spoiler alert: it didn't work and Helene died five months later).

Adolph's wife Pauline and three of Adolph's brothers also joined the CCAC, including brother Reverend August Ernst, already an ordained minister of the German Evangelical Association, also joined the CCAC. (August is listed with his family in the 1900 federal census as a resident "inmate" of the Dowie Institute, 1201 S. Michigan Ave., in Chicago.)

In 1905, Adolph and Pauline moved their family from Seattle to Zion City, Illinois, which was founded by Dowie as a socialist theocracy, along with several industries where the residents worked. Adolph died in 1907 when his son Louie was just 10 years old. After Adolph's death, Louis' mother Pauline lived with one of her daughters (one of Louie's sisters) in Spokane in 1920, then with another daughter in the 1930s in Oakland, California, where she died in 1947.

Louie attended Waukegan High School, as did Jack Benny (Benjamin Kubelsky), who was a couple of years older, and who was playing in the same theater as the young Marx Brothers. In 1911, Minnie, the Marx Brothers' mother, enjoyed Benny's violin playing and invited Benny to accompany her boys in their act. Benny's parents refused to let their son go on the road at 17, but it was the beginning of Benny's long friendship with the Marx Brothers, especially Zeppo, the youngest of the five brothers who took over the straight-man and romantic-lead roles from older brother Gummo.

Ernst family oral history says that Louie played in the same Chicago dance band as Benny at some point—placing us only three degrees of separation away from the Marx Brothers (some of my all-time heroes).

"From the moment I picked up your book until I laid it down, I was convulsed with laughter. Someday I intend reading it." —Groucho Marx
(Hopefully Groucho would have read this book)!

Grandpa Louie joined the U.S. Naval Reserve during World War I and was stationed at Chicago's Municipal Pier, later renamed Navy Pier, built by nationally renowned architect, Charles Sumner Frost. Louie was also certainly good with tools and may have learned carpentry from his father, or at least thought of it as his legacy. Louie reportedly also worked as a welder (a skill he may have learned in the Navy) building Chicago's O'Hare Airport as part of the war effort, which in 1942–43 was part of a manufacturing plant for Douglas C-54s.

In the early 1950s, Louie and local Wild Rose, Wisconsin, farmer, carpenter, and noted banjo player Harmon Mumbrue built Louie's lake cottage in Wild Rose, reportedly themselves. Being a packrat, remnants of Louie's memory live on at our family cottage in some of his hand tools, saws, cabinets, wading boots, and many "special boards" etched with his handwriting instructing us of the important purposes of each board.

Louie's wife, my grandmother, Laura Flossie Korbmacher, was born in Chicago on Aug. 4, 1899, and was an only child. Her parents, Charles and Hannah Korbmacher (her full birth name is Johanna Friederika Wilhelmina Klehm), were both born in Milwaukee to German immigrants who arrived in the 1840s and '50s, but moved to Hyde Park Township on the south side of Chicago. Charles' father was a cabinet maker and Hannah's was a shoemaker.

Charles was a clerk and cigar maker in Milwaukee and, later in Chicago, was a bottler at a brewery. Later he was a saloon keeper at 6759 S. May Street near Ogden Park in the Englewood neighborhood.

Charles Korbmacher died in 1910 when daughter Laura, my grandmother, was just 11 years old. Three years later, Laura's mother Hannah remarried another Charles, German-American Charles Malzow, who owned a delicatessen on Addison St., two blocks west of Wrigley Field. (Interestingly, three great-grandfathers on both sides of my family were named Charles.) They later changed their last name to Whitey, Charles Malzow's nickname, presumably thinking it would be good for business. Baby gift cards for grandchildren were signed "Grandma and Whitey."

Hannah died in 1952 (possibly of Alzheimer's) at the Chicago State Hospital, now the Chicago-Read Mental Health Center In 1954, two years later, Whitey drowned in the Chicago River. They are buried in unmarked graves. Reportedly, Grandpa Louie didn't think very highly of Whitey. He also didn't think much of cemeteries either, and forbade his family to visit Whitey's grave.

Collage of Laura Flossie Korbmacher Ernst photos

Family lore says that Laura worked in an office that Louie regularly called on as a salesman and he fell in love with her voice. After they married in 1920, they lived in apartments on North Robey Street (once called Fond du Lac Road, and later renamed Damen Avenue) in the Andersonville neighborhood near Rosehill Cemetery on the north side of Chicago. After their first two children were born (my Aunt Lois in 1922 and my father, Roger, in 1925), they moved in 1928 to a house half a block from Ebinger School in the quieter Chicago neighborhood of Edison Park.

Just eleven years earlier, Edison Park had been captured in a *Chicago Daily News* photo of a large sign displaying virulent anti-German sentiment during World War I.

In 1934, my dad's brother, Donald Klehm Ernst, was born almost ten years after my father. As the Great Depression dragged on and their budget was strained, the family moved in 1937 to a five-room upper duplex flat on Harlem Avenue near Higgins Road. In 1940, Louie and Laura rented a brick bungalow on Olcott Avenue in Edison Park, and then in 1956, bought a house, two doors down.

Children standing in front of an anti-German sign posted in the Edison Park neighborhood, 1917. (Photographer unknown)

* * * * *

Discrimination and hate come in all forms. By all peoples, races, creeds, and genders. Facing a new world war, this time against the Germans, Americans of German descent were now being ostracized and victimized. Ironically, Germans were not welcome in Edison Park, where my father's family and many other German-Americans had lived for decades.

It's hard not to think of the classic *Twilight Zone* episode, "The Monsters are Due on Maple Street," where families on a quiet, happy, suburban street, in the last calm and reflective moment, turn against each other, thinking they are being invaded by aliens. At the end, they of course learn that the monsters they fear are among themselves.

I never missed Rod Serling's show when I was young. The "sci-fi" of the show did not scare me, but through these fictional stories, I saw what prejudice can do. I was terrified by the thought of what these fictional neighbors, not very different from those I grew up with, would have done to me.

* * * * *

Louie rejected the Christian Catholic Apostolic Church (CCAC) when he moved away from Zion. He and Laura joined the Edison Park Evangelical & Reformed Church (later known as the Community Church of Edison Park), which represented a return to his family's German Evangelical Association roots.

Shortly after World War II ended, some of Louie's printing customers were so pleased with his work that they encouraged

Louie, Laura, Ann Marie and Roger Ernst
Me and my sister Barb, Easter candy and bunnies in baskets
Easter Day, circa 1953, Edison Park, Chicago

and helped him to start his own company. It was originally called Ernst & Company, Printers, but was changed later because Laura was concerned that on the phone it sounded like "Ernstine" Company (which, she thought, people would assume was Jewish).

I learned later in my life from my dearest and lifelong friend, Janet Downing, who grew up next door to my grandparents in Edison Park, as well as at her cottage on our same lake in Wild Rose, Wisconsin, (she even had a canoe named after her, the *Janet D*), knew them better than any of us. She had been told that my Grandpa Louie had actually played cornet professionally in the 1930s jazz clubs of Chicago.

Louie and Laura were undoubtedly influenced by their parents' attitudes, and may have passed some of those down to their children, who either accepted or rebelled against them. I didn't know them well enough to consider how they would have responded to me and my identity, but sadly, I'm afraid they would not have understood or accepted me for who I was. That has always been a dark thought for me.

In 1975, Louie died of a heart attack in his Ernst Printing Company office at the age of 78. As my father Roger always said, "He died with his boots on." Louie's wife Laura lived six more years.

I echo my cousin John Geertz-Larson's sentiments: "As a male grandchild, I was expected to perform manual labor at Ernst Printing Company on a number of Saturdays in my late tweens. The main tasks I remember were sweeping the hard-wood floors with pink sweeping compound, and moving pallets of paper stock around. If those were recruiting visits, they failed—but I still get nostalgic at the smell of color ink on shiny paper, and I've been known to wear a rubber band or two on my wrist as an homage."

I still have pink sweeping compound in my shoes and ink in my blood. I also wear those popular rubber wristbands, probably a vestige of my childhood and tribute to Grandpa Louie. And note that my grandfather was in a dress as an infant. Maybe that's why I am transgender today!

Ann Marie Ernst

My mother, Anne Marie Ernst (nee Smith), was soft-spoken, stoic, kind, non-judgmental, and always supportive, an archetypal product of the post-war, 1950s housewife. She was and always will be stunning in appearance. My mother was also extremely talented. In addition to having raised seven children, she worked successfully as an interior decorator in the Chicago area, and always maintained an active social life.

My mother was the primary source for my life-long happiness, fortitude, and positive attitude. I have never heard her utter a negative word or even cry. The one exception to that would be when she was pregnant (I don't remember her ever *not* being pregnant), and came home from a doctor's appointment on a very cold, blizzardy Chicago morning—on a day when all five of us kids were laid up sick with the flu. She had just found out that she was having twins and burst into tears when she got home. She was so upset she had to have one of my sisters call my father to tell him. We've all subsequently recovered from the flu, and I think she has adjusted to her twins. But after that, I don't think she planned on having any more kids.

Regarding my gender identity, although my mother certainly knew when I was born about my intersex status, and now knows that I am a woman, when I was growing up, she always had a modicum knowledge level of, or perhaps interest, in my gender identity. I suspect she was either too shy, stoic and/or Catholic to address it, and just too busy raising her seven kids and building her interior design business. This was not the kind of thing she would have felt comfortable talking about.

I once asked her how babies were made. She said that's something that grown-ups do. And I was 40 years old when I asked her! Thus, I always felt that if I ever had been bold enough to talk with my mom about my gender identity, I think my mom would have been totally OK with it as long as I didn't put soft-drink glasses on her coffee table without a coaster. That was my mom. If I had asked her, "What's normal, Mom?" I think her response might have been, "It's just a setting on the dryer, Honey."

I had wonderful grandparents on both sides, but I was probably influenced most by my maternal grandmother, Alice Cecilia Smith. My grandmother was quite lively, chaotic, gifted, unpredictable, and very opinionated, particularly about her

Edmund J. Smith, the "gentle grandfather:"

husband Edmund (my gentle grandfather)—who, according to my grandmother, was always doing everything wrong, at least from her perspective. His ongoing answer was always the same, *"I can't complain. Wouldn't do any good if I did!"*

Interestingly, I also have fleeting memories of her that seem to have been repressed until this moment as I write about them, and particularly related to the topic of gender. For example, when I was quite young, I spent my weekends with her; for some reason, she had clearly identified me as a girl. She would whisper to me that I was "her little girl." She often dressed me in vintage blouses and dresses, as was the formal custom for females and males born in her era of the 1890s. I spent many long days in Grandma Smith's art studio—which I loved, where she taught me to paint with oils—and on the beaches of Lake Michigan.

We visited the summer homes of her gilded-class friends and their families, such as Milton J. Holloway, known for developing Milk Duds and the Slo-Poke candy bar; and Paul Galvin and Virginia (Galvin Piper) who, after many failed attempts, finally got a radio to work in a car without it exploding, thus inventing the mass production of car radios, founded a little company around it, and called it Motorola.

Virginia Galvin was a close friend of my grandmother's and someone I would see often on our visits, teas, and other soirees. After Paul's death, Virginia married Jack Piper, and after his passing, went on to become a significant philanthropist in Scottsdale, Arizona. I remember her as a woman of incredible style and grace. She was also an amazing letter-writer, which I think taught me more than anything else the value of letter-writing, particularly thank-you notes. Her legacy is captured in a YouTube video, *The Story of Virginia Galvin Piper: A Dedicated Life*. For me, it's emotionally striking to occasionally hear NPR program sponsorship credits about her extraordinary hospitals and other charitable legacies in the Scottsdale region so many years later in my life.

Being raised among my grandmother's friends provided deep values and broad perspectives, yet also a bit of contrast of the vastly different economic worlds her friends lived in compared to ours that I could not even begin to comprehend. Even in those days, I knew my inner feminine persona had to be kept hidden, for it was unlikely that society would understand or accept me.

Oddly, my grandmother did! She was surely the only person in my life who did. My grandmother played dolls with me, bringing out her fancy antique dolls, and held tea parties with me on her fancy china, and other girly things. I was living the wonderful life of a little girl—at least on weekends. This, of course, seemed perfectly normal to me and resonated with my female brain. I had nothing else to compare it to. I was engaged in the moment. I was happy.

Grandma Alice and I also danced a lot. We would dress up in dance costumes, often dresses. She would swing me around the room and sing along and spoof the popular early Rock-n-Roll tunes of the era, like *Nothing but a Hound Dog* and *Rock Around the Clock*. The tunes belted out of a small, white Motorola AM radio with its big, red tuning knob. I will forever cherish those memories with her.

My grandmother's values were deeply rooted in her own childhood, primarily shaped by the Gilded Age of the early 20th century, an era of American inventiveness, mass-produced automobiles, radios, flappers, a chicken in every pot, the Depression, and I would surmise—a pretense of still living in the long-past, gentry-class world shaped by her father and my great-grandfather, Charles Addison Wightman.

Born on October 11, 1861, in Kenosha, Wisconsin, Charles Wightman was the son of Addison Porter and Sarah Jane (Richards) Wightman. In 1885, he earned a Bachelor of Philosophy degree at Northwestern University in the rapidly growing

Charles A. Wightman,
my great-grandfather

prairie town of Evanston, immediately annexing Chicago to the north. After the 1871 Chicago Fire, many city dwellers looked to the suburbs for new homes to escape from the poverty and crowding of Chicago. Evanston soon became known as the "City of Homes." Architects began designing homes and the city soon was renowned for its quiet, tree-lined streets and fine housing. Charles was very much a part of this life and became a very successful real estate developer, insurance broker, and patron of the arts and architecture.

On March 28, 1894 He married Cecilia Agnes Daley, (his second wife). Charles and Cecilia lived in a sprawling home at 1735 Wesley Avenue in Evanston (still standing), where they raised their four daughters: Catherine Sarah, Margaret Mary, Alice Cecilia (my grandmother), and Rosemary Caroline.

Charles Whiteman was also a contemporary, friend, and patron of many legendary architects, including Louis Sullivan, John Root, Daniel Burnham, Lawrence Perkins, and Frank Lloyd Wright, who together formed the basis of "Chicago Style" architecture at a time of burgeoning expansion to accommodate a surge in population wrought by the Great Fire of 1871.

Much later, likely in the 1920s or 1930s, Charles adopted a fifth daughter in Chicago name Mary "Cele" Cecilia Wightman (Briggs), whom he raised along with his much older daughters, Catherine and Margaret, in another sprawling home in Bel Air, California (owned later by actor Vic Morrow).

Charles Whiteman was an avid reader and book collector, and among many other things, was known for his collection of fine paintings and hundreds of rare books. He also was associated with P.F. Volland, the company founded by Paul Frederick Volland in 1908. (Volland was later shot and killed by Vera Trepagnier in a business dispute on May 5, 1919 in the Volland offices.)

Volland published the prints of the American artist Jules Guerin (1866-1946), whose renderings captured many well-known American landmarks of his day, including the spirit of Daniel Burnham's 1909 *Plan of Chicago*, of which Jules Guérin created several birds-eye views for the full-color document, which was printed in lavish book form.

Apart from running his company, the Evanston Bond & Mortgage Company at 1606 Chicago Avenue, Charles Wightman was an enthusiastic collector of religious art. He also owned and

Wightman Memorial Art Gallery, 2nd floor of Bond Hall, ca. 1925.

ran the University Art Shop, Inc. (circa 1906-1921), an art publishing house in the landmark 208 University Building (1604-1606 Chicago Avenue) in downtown Evanston, which published the Guerin prints.

Wightman was also known for establishing the Wightman Memorial Art Gallery, located in the Library of the University of Notre Dame, after he had donated 108 paintings of religious subjects in memory of his late (and second) wife, Cecilia, to the college in 1924.

I never knew my great-grandfather, but I understand that his wealth dwindled significantly primarily due to the Depression. The donation and distribution of his formidable artwork collection went to extended family members and much of the rest he donated to the Notre Dame Art Museum.

This extended backdrop of my family and its legacy further conveys the society and era in which I grew up. It was traditional and typical of these kinds of families and standards, values, and social norms. For me, it was solid and safe. It was all I ever knew. As happy and harmonious it was on the outside, however, it was incongruous with the person I was on the inside. It would have been impossible to ever reveal my innermost secret. I was alone and sad about that, not even knowing the long journey that stood before me.

5. When Winston Tasted Good...The 1950s

Growing up in the midst and adventures of the post-war economic boom and prosperity of the Golden Age of Capitalism —an age of urban sprawl, suburban flight, the invention of shopping malls, drive-in movies, Elvis Presley, Ed Sullivan, and 15-cent hamburgers, I rarely thought much about my little "secret."

The G.I. Bill financed a well-educated workforce for our fathers. The middle class swelled, as did the GDP and overall productivity. It was a time of unusually sustained growth and suburban sprawl supporting full employment in America.

Many of our values were shaped by the novelty of television, its inexhaustible, cheery commercials, and the great promises of their products, assuring us that our lives would be perfect, and

TV adds so much to family happiness

that true happiness could be attained, if only we could just get our clothes brighter and our teeth whiter.

If our family life and 1950s values were not reinforced enough by our gender-specific toys (girls to play with dolls, boys to play with diggers and footballs), it was further reflected, confirmed, and shaped by the plots of our three-channeled, black-and-white, rabbit-eared, fuzzy Motorola console TV, broadcasting our TV friends such as *Kukla, Fran & Ollie*, *Leave It to Beaver*, *Ozzie & Harriet*, *I Love Lucy*, and *Dick Clark's American Bandstand*, to name a few.

This included the life-validating values permanently etched into our brains about the importance of having bright,

shiny, white teeth, making us, *wonder where the yellow went when we brushed our teeth with Pepsodent,* as the memorable commercials ran in our heads for life...

... or, how Wonder Bread could build strong bodies in eight ways. And our amazement as to how the *Pop, Pop, Fizz, Fizz* of Alka-Seltzer could cure any stomach ailment.

We also were continually inundated with the nutritional values and healing powers of health foods, such as Oscar Meyer hotdogs in the WienerMobile, Bosco "chocolate," Velveeta "cheese," and orange-flavored Tang, which had the ability to sustain astronauts in orbit for years. Of course, we were sometimes treated with other health-food favorites like Hostess Twinkies and Marshmallow Fluff. Yum!

More detrimental, as we now know in hindsight, many

sponsors included the tobacco companies such as Camel cigarettes (so glad doctors liked and smoked these the most), Lucky Strikes (the choice of my father—actually, late father, due to emphysema), and Winston's, which always assured us that *Winston Tastes Good, Like a Cigarette Should* (proper grammar withstanding).

Amazingly, we all survived these "health-food" products. If I hadn't already been convinced of the intrinsic nutritional values of all these important products by then, ironically, it was sure to be reinforced as all these brands returned to my life many years later. I worked in Chicago as a commercial jingle writer for radio and TV ads in the heyday of television jingles, being one of the people who composed and produced the musical score for the part when the announcer would say, "We'll return after these important messages."

That was me! My music! At least some of it. And much later, I ended up serving in senior levels at large public relations firms in New York. With these early media underpinnings, no wonder I was destined to eventually work on Madison Avenue.

6. *Superboy / Supergirl*

When I was about five years old or so, I experienced a defining moment in my gender journey, reading in my tent sturdily pitched on the lake shore of our family summer cottage in Wisconsin—a *Superboy* comic book story (the teenage incarnation from Smallville, the boyhood version of my all-time hero, the Man of Steel himself, along with his super-powered canine, Krypto).

At that time in my life, my three life heroes were Santa Claus, Jesus Christ, and Superman—with the latter trumping the other two because he could fly without the need of a sleigh (although he did a have a considerable problem with Kryptonite) and Jesus, who couldn't fly at all, and seemed to have severe identity issues dealing with his father and his holy ghost.

In one particular adventure, Superboy woke up one morning as Supergirl. But in a comic book, anything could happen, of course, so his ever-doting, no-nonsense, moral-infusing mother Ma Kent on the Kansas plains—who had always encouraged Clark to use his super powers for the betterment of humanity— simply helped her now-daughter become Supergirl in a typical, no-nonsense, Kansas-like way. (And hey, I don't say that in a disparaging way, as I'm a University of Kansas Jayhawk—*Rock Chalk. Jay Hawk!*—as the venerable Jayhawk cheer goes.)

When I read the story, I thought, "Why couldn't this happen to me? Just wake up as a girl?" But later in that episode, Supergirl was hit by a bolt of Kryptonite or some such force, was brought back to her senses and transformed back into a boy. (I thought, "Too bad for her!") This was how I perceived the world of gender, even at five.

7. Sports

Sports were hard for me. As a male, everyone expects you to play something. To excel. To compete. To win. That is how you were judged.

By the time I was seven years old, though, I remember wishing I could be just like all the other girls. Something just seemed right about who and what they were. I enjoyed everything about them. I had many "play dates," but primarily with girls. During recess, when the boys played ball sports or tag, I always played with the girls on the swings. This dissonance was only reinforced throughout my childhood as I was continually confronted with "guy" sports.

My dad was a typical suburban sports enthusiast of the times. I remember avoiding testosterone-infused sports games–likely a great disappointment to my jock father, of course. He never understood why I "never played football with the guys," or hockey. Baseball. Basketball. Boxing. Wrestling. Or any guy sport for that matter. Although I did love tennis, gymnastics, swimming, badminton, and figure skating, but really, how guy-like are those sports? At least in that era.

I "fondly" remember fall weekends of backyard practice drills with my dad hurtling footballs at me while I was attired like a sardine, head to toe, in full football regalia. But with my female instincts and brain wiring innately inside of me, all I could think was, "Do I look fat in these pads?"

8. The Mitt

I spent summers being banished to right field in baseball games—kind of a Purgatory on earth, where the marginal players were sent to prevent any serious damage to the team.

This humiliating experience was further compounded and intensified when the way-more macho guys assembled to draft their teams. After they chose and fought over their "star" players, they would then say, "OK. I'll take Ernst." Clearly a charity case.

Even worse, I was mitt-challenged. Since we never saw real brands in my large family, we always ended up with off-brands that no one had ever heard of. Other kids always got brand-new mitts every year from the then-upscale Ray's Sport Shop in town, where you could always find top-of-the-line equipment with names like Wilson, Rawlings, and Spalding – enough to outfit the Cubs, Blackhawks, or Da Bears in style.

But not for me. Dad found me an off-brand mitt at a discount store. One day, my mitt arrived in an unmarked brown box. I put it on. It was flat as a pancake and stiff as a board. My dad said to just "work it" until it got flexible. So, I worked it diligently for weeks, day and night. I lathered it in 3-in-1 oil. Boiled it in salt water. Baked it. Froze it. Jumped on it. Ran over it with my bike. Dropped it out of the third-story attic window. Squeezed it in a vice for weeks. But it never budged. Still hard as a rock.

Then one day, adorned with my new (but still flat) mitt, I went to play in a softball game, and as always, was banished to right field. That said, I actually never minded the solitude since it kept me in a world of my own and far from the goings-on of the game.

I really didn't have to do anything since my teammates counted on me to not do anything. Then, one fateful day, Steve, a

GLENCOE BASEBALL LEAGUE
NATIONAL LEAGUE
1962 CHAMPIONS

powerful left-handed hitter came up to the plate. We were all warned to go back. Way back. To add insult to injury, the game was tied at the top of the ninth, bases were loaded, and emotions were high. Unlike me, my teammates really cared whether or not they won or lost. And they wanted to win. Badly.

Fulfilling my team's worse fears, Steve belted the ball miles into the stratosphere toward right field—my field. The team gasped in horror. The ball seemed to disappear into the brightly gleaming, sun-drenched cosmos forever. Then, as it re-entered the earth's orbit, everyone could see it hurtling directly toward me! Dead center toward my unbranded, flat, non-budging mitt, which seemed to possess a strong magnetic pull like a laser beam attracting the ball.

I knew this was a make-or-break sports career moment for me, a defining moment that would forever determine if I played sports ever again, at least in America. It might potentially catapult me into local sports fame, fortune, and lore—or permanently banish me forever from all sports.

Sure enough, the ball came squarely and directly to my mitt like a heat-seeking, guided SCUD missile. I couldn't miss. No one could miss—unless you had a flat, unbending, discount-store, flat baseball mitt. The ball hit my mitt dead on with a thud, but unfortunately, the mitt functioned more like a Ping-Pong paddle, repelling that first, fast-served ball. The ball practically knocked me over. It bounced off my mitt and onto the ground, rolling about 20 feet in front of me.

I knew what to do! I ran to the ball and threw it as hard as I could, but managed to get it only about 15 feet toward the infield and less than halfway to the second baseman. He frantically ran to the ball and threw it precisely at the speed of light to the pitcher, who by then, was covering home plate.

But it was too late. It arrived just in time to see the runners slide into home, assuring a solid win. For the other team. This was a bad end of the season for our team. As well as my baseball career. And my entire sports career for that matter. And life as a boy.

9. Bless Me, Father, Music, and Chicago

Since my childhood was enriched in part with a Jewish culture, it had a profound influence on me and my identity, impacted by Shabbat traditions and enhanced with enough delicatessen, gefilte fish, kreplach soup, lox and bagels, bialies, and blintzes to feed a kibbutz. My life was regularly sprinkled like incense with a regular dose of Hebrew and Latin. And because most of my friends were Jewish, I assumed I was Jewish, too. This seemed to culminate in enough Jewish guilt and culture for me to live on a kibbutz.

I was lucky to have a best friend growing up. I'm still as close with him today as we were as kids. His name is Clay. Clay Frohman to be exact. I met him in second grade when our teacher called him off the playground and back into class after recess. I remember being struck by hearing the name "Clay" for the first time, having previously known it only as the stuff you make art with.

It goes beyond the scope of this book to talk about how much Clay (the person) has been and still is part of my life, but all the usual things kids do, we did—baseball, birthday parties, swimming, overnights, camping, vacationing, school, concerts, double dating, stereo system shopping, and lusting for stereo gear and musical instruments, and later, played a lot of music since we formed several quintessential budding bands reminiscent of the 1960s and '70s musical era.

We performed in our band during our college summers in Chicago. We also "experimented" together (mildly, in case any authorities are reading this) with the popular hallucinatory diversions of the times. Clay was—and is—extremely talented as both a performing musician, singer / songwriter, and professionally, is a gifted Hollywood screenwriter.

Clay always said that when he grew up, he wanted to be a screenwriter. Although I'm not certain he ever grew up, he did indeed become a very successful screenwriter and still does that today (and, of course, still plays and sings in bands in Los Angeles).

I had always known Clay was destined for greatness. Once, he staged a massive and impressive show in sixth grade called *The Planets*, with artwork, posters, models, music, and lots of content that rivaled NASA or Gustave Holst's efforts.

Another time, Clay staged a massive play in his backyard, the production ambitiously being a reenactment of the Battle of the Alamo. This is difficult to do with about 50 fourth graders running around dressed as Texas Defenders or Mexican troops, all likely coerced into service to act—mostly due to Clay's mother's chocolate chip cookies for all their efforts. I'm confident we will always remember the Alamo, since I'm sure Clay's backyard play will someday be optioned soon for a movie—if he can track down all his actors. And his mom's cookies.

I particularly loved Clay's parents and his maternal grand-mother, who regularly stuffed me with beet borscht, bagels and blintzes—she was the Jewish grandmother I never had.

And Clay's mother, Vola—my second mother (if not my first)—doubled as our band's press agent and photographer. The

Vola and David Frohman, Clay's parents

Annie Leibovitz of our community, she was always armed with her Kodak point-and-shoot, hand-held Brownie camera, ready to capture a rare spark of brilliance emulating out of our ragtag electric guitars, drums, and sax of our fledgling rock band, *The Vibranauts*.

We were four kids with crew cuts, white turtlenecks and black pants, loosely modeled after the rock-and-surf bands of the era—Bill Haley and His Comets and the American surf band, The Surfaris, with their memorable instrumental (and only) hit *Wipe Out*, all of which was happening around the pre-dawn days of the Beatles. (Hey, they stole our thunder. "You don't understand. I coulda had class. I coulda been a contender. I coulda been somebody" as Terry Malloy so forlornly stated.)

Our folk/jazz/blues band was not my first foray into music. I had started playing clarinet when I was around six years old, participating in the traditional band and orchestra programs typical of most elementary schools. My first "performance" was around third grade, playing in the town's Memorial Day Parade marching band, uniformed in all-white outfits and red belts (borrowed from the volunteer crossing guard patrol students).

However, that event was a bit traumatic in that one of my borrowed shoes from my father, which was too big, fell off. I tried to retrieve it, but the show must go on and any attempt to reach down and get it was thwarted by trombone valves going up my posterior.

Other performance "traumas" included getting stuck on a sailboat on Lake Michigan due to no wind before a graduation ceremony at my high school, which resulted in my having to hitchhike to the event with a large baritone saxophone in tow, not to mention my sunburned skin.

Another time, I drove 40 miles to a major jazz band competition in Kansas City with other musicians on a cold, wintery morning. We put our horns in the trunk of the car, while Tommy the Trumpeter navigated the car via a small, cleared hole on the window. The car lacked windshield wipers, among other vital car parts. We arrived just as the curtain was going up. I was to play lead alto sax.

As fate would have it, when I got into position under the glaring gaze of the band director, I realized my sax was frozen and all the pads had popped out. Since the 2,000-some people in the audience were mostly other musicians, the director asked the crowd if anyone could lend me a sax. Some poor Army band guy walked up to the stage and handed me his $6,000 Selmer Mark VI alto sax.

As I grabbed it by the neck, the horn came apart and bounced on the stage, exploding into springs, keys, and pads. The audience was aghast. So, me being me, I grabbed the mike and asked, "Could I have another one?"

Most of my performances were less ill-fated. I continued to write music and play clarinet, flute, and sax in many bands and orchestras, pit bands, parties, and events throughout high school.

One of my formative experiences was becoming the music director of our high-school talent show called *Lagniappe.* With a legacy going back to the school's earliest days, and a show touting past stars like Ann-Margret, Bruce Dern, Charlton Heston, and Rock Hudson, to name but a few, by then with a student population of 6,558, the show had become a cultural signature of the community. With all my friends and extended family attending opening night, along with some of the celebrities who came to see it, the expectations were high and the pressure was intense.

This whole experience put a lot of stress on me, having done it both junior and senior years. I was responsible for composing, arranging, and conducting the orchestra and choir, along with other student composers and performers, and working year-long with fellow board members, who wrote and produced the overall show.

Opening night, I was to come out of the orchestra pit stage door, illuminated by a follow spot, decked out in a tux with baton in hand. But after a year of preparation, I froze in the moment like a deer in the headlights. I couldn't go out the door. It was only because Heidi, the show's choral director, literally pushed me out the door. I stumbled out to the podium and started the show. From there on, after a few deep breaths comforted by the then-familiar fanfare of the overture, I was OK. By my college years, I continued similar musical endeavors, performed and studied composition, but with much less trauma.

In the summers back in Chicago, Clay and I continued our band and changed the name to Soft Landing, one of those hip, whimsical band names of the era (although it didn't help our booking prospects as much as we had hoped).

Being Transgender

In 1920, critic H. L. Mencken wrote in *The Nation* that Chicago was the "Literary Capital of the United States." By the 1970s, live folk music in Chicago was particularly in its prime, where most every night, audiences had a wide choice of venues to choose from, easily found in the bible of alternative journalism and coverage of the arts, particularly film, music, and theater: *The Chicago Reader* (or ЯEADER).

I don't know if Clay and I fully appreciated the historical and cultural context into which we were parachuted, nor would we have dared to enter the fray if we did know of the deep cultural and musical legacy associated with Chicago. We were at the tail end of a former grimy industrial city built on meat packing, railroads, printing, graft, and grunge—a city long since in transition to becoming a major capital of gleaming architecture, diverse neighborhoods, music and film festivals, cafes, and international business. However, in my opinion, Chi-Town has still not shaken much of its underbelly of crime, grit, and blight.

By the time we performed in Chicago, it had a long and rich history of distinguished and timeless musicians, artists, writers, and performers. This is recounted in the works of poets like Nelson Algren in his *Chicago: City on the Make,* and Carl Sandburg's legendary line, *City of Big Shoulders.* Books and authors, like Saul Alinsky's *Rules for Radicals* and many others—Saul Bellows, Jane Addams, Richard Wright, and Upton Sinclair's *The Jungle,* and one of my favorites, Erik Larson's *Devil in the White City.*

Chicago has also had a long tradition of folk musicians, like Big Bill Broonzy, Bob Gibson, brothers Ed and Fred Holstein, Win Stracke, and Art Thieme, among others. Blues greats emerged as well at the birthplace of Chicago Blues, the historic and ethnically diverse, open-air Maxwell Street Market, and all over the city—such as Paul Butterfield, Bo Didley, Willie Dixon, Jimmy Johnson, Otis Rush, Otis Span, "Hound Dog" Taylor, Muddy Waters, Junior Wells, and Howlin' Wolf.

Probably my all-time favorite blues performer was Estella "Mama" Yancey (youtube.com/watch?v=jw9tMRhKEak), whom I had the joy and privilege to meet and regularly hear her play in the private home of Chicago's blues-boogie-jazz pianist and long-recognized music treasure, Erwin Helfer (youtube.com/watch?v=uvhfTauSmUc), my neighbor at the time on Magnolia Street. He still resides in the small brick house, dwarfed by the Lincoln Park brownstones, DePaul University, and area high-rises.

There are also, of course, many jazz legends: Benny Goodman, Von Freeman, Ramsey Lewis, Art Hodes, Herbie Hancock, Sonny Stitt, Joe Daley, Mel Torme, and Dinah Washington; and not to forget jazz/rock bands such as Earth, Wind & Fire and Chicago.

Chicago could also be funny, producing comedians like Bob Newhart, John and Jim Belushi, Dan Aykroyd, and Bill Murray—to name just a few of the many legendary artists of our time. Chicago culture was well chronicled and reinforced by journalist Mike Royko and his book, *Boss*, and notably, and another favorite of mine, author, historian, actor, and broadcaster Studs

Terkel with his book *Working,* and at the time, his morning radio show on Chicago's WFMT.

Clay and I did have a modicum level of fame as we participated in the Chicago folk music scene of the early 1970s, not realizing we were playing on stages, folk clubs, and coffee houses with rising stars of the era, like John Prine, Steve Goodman, and Bonnie Koloc, among others, confirmed (at least on our minds) by seeing our name on the marquee of undistinguished folk clubs: the "It's Here" in Rogers Park (albeit in small type) but big enough to be captured by the lens of our press agent, Clay's mom.

We also were "discovered" by some audio engineers at CBS's WBBM (News Radio 780), who recorded us in their radio studio at night after the live broadcast shows by "ping-ponging" our mono audio tracks. Essentially, this was a poor man's multi-tracking system that bounced our tracks back and forth from machine to machine as we added tracks. However, the music, of course, degraded in each pass, like a copy of a copy, until we could no longer hear the first track. But we were blinded by the exuberant and dedicated engineer, who regularly exclaimed when he heard us, "It's AstroJazz!" being convinced his ship had come in and we were his ticket to being the "next big thing."

Unfortunately for all of us, we weren't. It wasn't. Regardless of our well-intended efforts, Clay and I are still very close friends today, where no amount of time's passing has ever diminished how much we care for each other. True friends are rare, and best friends even rarer.

I have continued to perform and write music ever since. Looking back, I was lucky to have studied with various teachers and performers available to me at the time who provided significant guidance that I have incorporated into who I am today as a musician. As time has ticked forward, I now realize that some of these teachers were or have become highly influential music legends of our time.

I had a few lessons on tenor sax with the revered avant-garde American jazz tenor saxophonist Joe Daly in Chicago; I got to know American jazz baritone saxophonist and composer Pepper Adams at a jazz summer camp, where one night we sat down at a piano and composed a song together; I played alto sax in a "head band" under American composer, conductor, jazz musician, arranger and author Bill Russo; and I studied jazz piano with the amazing performer, leader, composer Bob Ravenscroft in Scottsdale, Arizona (darkwoodbrew.org/bob-ravenscroft/).

Probably the most fun I've ever had in music was with my partner, Roye Bourke, the other half of Bourke & Ernst music. We first met in Scottsdale, Arizona, where we connected immediately. Roye is a very talented singer, songwriter, guitar player, with a strong and feisty spirit—and she's a gorgeous woman. We started out writing advertising jingles in Phoenix, and as our lives took us to other locales, continued writing and producing music for all kinds of media from Los Angeles to New York. Later, we worked with the ever-talented Eric Bikales, an old college friend, now one of the top studio musicians and composers in Nashville.

Today, I still compose and play clarinet, flute, and saxophone in a variety of community bands, orchestras, quartets, and jazz groups.

It's difficult to identify just one "best friend" from childhood, as I was lucky to have many very wonderful and close friends. But one more childhood friend who I was and still am very close to is Charles or "Chip" Mack, who, when I wasn't discovering the joys and challenges of childhood with Clay, Chip was always with me as we explored other life adventures together. All the "firsts" of life—learning to ride a bike, first days at school, science projects, music, scouting, sailing, sports, hiking, family vacations, and dating.

Some shared adventures that are indelibly and permanently etched into our brains, include: a time when we were arrested for

Chip (back row, 3rd from left), Clay (front row, 2nd from left), me (somewhere) and other scouts

climbing on the town water works looking for our softball, resulting in a sentence of essays about what we did wrong and why would not do that again, along with two weeks raking up dead alewives (very smelly fish) on the beach. Another was the morning we sailed to high school on Lake Michigan but were four hours late due to lack of wind (another essay). And another was a three-day and night drive from Chicago to Breckenridge, Colorado to help a family move in return for two weeks of free skiing. We have always been there for each other during the chapter changes and challenges of life.

* * * * *

My mother was an "obligatory" Catholic. No discussion. We just went to CHURCH. And unless you were a 2000-year-old Roman, it was difficult to make heads or tails out of the all-Latin masses spouted by old priests with their backs turned to the congregation.

On cold, dark, snowy, windy Chicago Saturday nights, my mother drove us all to confession. This was a surreal, Kafkaesque experience, locking us in a black box talking to an invisible voice. The church was large, cold, and marble. Very quiet, with just a few people mumbling in the pews.

But once in the confessional, it was all business. We were there to confess our sins of the week. That was serious stuff. When the priest regularly asked me each week like clockwork what I had done wrong and I sheepishly replied, "Nothing," he said to reach deep into my soul and find something. Once I said, "Look, I'm only five years old. What could I have done since last week?"

Under intense pressure to start sinning, the next week I said, "Bless me, Father, for I have sinned, and I pulled the hair of one of my sisters." He said that was bad and to get down on my knees and say some Our Father's and Hail Mary's for penance.

The next week, I came in with a lot of guilt and this time said, "You know how I said I pulled my sister's hair? Well, I didn't. I lied under the pressure to start sinning."

He said, "Now you've done it. You've now committed an official sin!"

He threw the Book of Penance at me and gave me a whole Rosary's worth of work to do. It was then and there, at Sacred Heart Church in Hubbard Woods, where I got into the rhythm of sinning and being bad ever since.

On Sunday mornings, we were schlepped off to a morning of catechism class and Catholic mass. Of course, all in Latin (not my native tongue), with real nuns and hard metal rulers. But even with their Knuckle Abuse Syndrome in action, at the same time (clearly bi-polar women), they would whisper to me softly and ask, "Did you ever consider becoming a nun?"

I would reply, "Not for a millionth of a second, but I'm all ears. What's in it for me?"

I would ask, "How will I know if I'm nun material?"

They said not to worry—I would get a calling from God.

Well, I didn't check my cellphone this morning, but so far, not a word. So, any sense of "struggling" with inner gender identity was drowned out by the challenges of getting through a day of chaos in a nine-person "army" consisted of my family and ridden with pools of Catholic guilt.

As a former Catholic, I think I choked on too much holy water and it went to my brain. Wasn't my thing. I gave up Lent for Lent. And the whole religion thing. I took four years of Latin in high school, but it didn't help much with my spiritual journey. I guess I had hoped to travel to Latin America someday, but was later told they don't speak Latin there and to try Italy. But after learning that Latin was no longer spoken there either, I asked what they speak today, so I switched to Italian in college, hoping they don't change the language again.

And with all my double Jewish and Catholic guilt—forever worried about lying or sinning due to the ongoing threat of severe penance—this only further exacerbated intense, real pain from my deep secret that I could never let out. That was something I thought I could never tell the truth about.

10. Just the Facts (of Life), Ma'am

The other aspect of growing up Catholic, at least in our family, was that we never, ever spoke about sex. It just didn't exist. As far as we all knew, we were immaculately conceived. Dolls were all anatomically *in*correct. This all came to a head, when as the oldest child, my parents apparently decided it was time for me to be told the "Facts of Life."

My dad was assigned that dreadful and uncomfortable task. I knew this was about to happen because my parents were acting strange, and things were different. Very different.

I was about twelve years old. However, as result of a childhood of playgrounds, friends, books, and *Playboy* magazines ("borrowed" from my dad's "secret" hiding place stuffed under his bed), I thought I had a fairly reasonable degree of understanding of the "FACTS." (This despite my friend Chip explaining to me that newborn babies extruded from between women's breasts). Made perfect sense at the time.

Regardless, the "Talk" still had to be done. This was as uncomfortable for my dad as it was for me.

It was apparently decided for the deed to take place "UpNort" at our summer cottage, out of earshot of anyone who might be negatively affected or psychologically injured.

The first sign that something was off-kilter was that my dad said, "Let's go fishing. On another lake."

This was different because we didn't fish. And we never went to other lakes. However, we got up around 4 a.m. the next morning. This was different too, since we rarely got up before 9 in the morning. He woke me up in the darkness of the early morning and made me some coffee—something I had never had before. That, too, was different. I might as well have mainlined it. At least I was wide-awake and highly buzzed from my first-ever dose of caffeine.

After we struggled in the pre-dawn darkness to get the rowboat tied down on the top of the family nine-passenger

Mercury station wagon, we drove through the darkness and thick mist of the pre-dawn morning.

No words were uttered. I had never been so awake in my life as I stared into the darkness, nor heard so much silence, until we arrived at a long, winding, sandy road leading to another lake. Twin Lake to be specific. A lake with no cottages. No people. And probably no fish. I suspect this was to prevent our lake from being polluted with any words about procreation.

At the shorefront of the barren lake, in complete silence, we dismounted the rowboat from the Mercury's roof and put it on the water's edge, filled it with fishing poles, slimy worms, the requisite life preservers, and a tackle box, and launched the now well-equipped fishing vessel.

As the sun rose in the east, we purposefully rowed to the center of the lake. Dad and I sat there for an hour or so with not a single bite or any words being spoken. (This is good because neither of us would have known what to do with a fish dangling on the end of a line anyway.)

The silence was deafening and the awkwardness painful. Finally, my father looked at me awkwardly, but with great sincerity and intensity, and with a sense of anticipation and well-rehearsed words, said, "Son, do you know where babies come from?"

I looked up and replied with great conviction and fortitude, "Yes."

He replied with a look of relief on his brow and said mono-syllabically, "Good."

With that, we stowed all the fishing gear, rowed back to the shore, reversed everything we had done that morning, went home, and the topic was never broached again.

Never.

That's what it was like, at least for me, growing up in a large Catholic family. And I don't even like fish. And I would add, it would hardly have been an opportune time to discuss gender dysphoria.

11. Wearing Dresses

From the time I hit puberty, I knew I was a girl inside. But of course, I didn't have any role models from whom to learn how to express these constant feelings, and I had never heard of the word *transgender*. I don't know if all of my family knew, but I suspect my parents saw me as the pink sheep of the family.

I lived in constant fear of anyone ever knowing about the real me. Such a discovery would destroy our perfect 1950s family and "Gee, Beav'! What would Ward say?" parallel family sensibilities. So, I tried my best to suppress my feelings, hoping they would just go away.

I also liked performing on "stage" (an old skid) in the music "pit" (a stairway) under the Klieg lights (my dad's camera lights) and "proscenium" (sheets from the dryer) set up in our basement for our plays with my sisters and friends. The other boys in the play would complain about the costumes, saying things like,

"Why do I have to wear makeup and dresses? I don't want to wear dresses!" Somehow, I felt obligated to feign a similar sense of disappointment.

Needless to say, I loved the feeling of makeup and how my eyes looked with eyeliner. It also was fun wearing the tights, dresses, and wigs from the large costume box. However, I felt terribly conflicted, thinking that maybe my ever-present, strong sense of femininity might simply go away. But it didn't. It just got worse, and I became more aware of my agonizing condition when puberty hit. I watched as my body grew—and increasingly with female characteristics.

It was around age 12 that I knew something was out of sync between my body, inner sense of identity, and the confirmed gender identities of my friends solidifying all around me. It was then that I started questioning and putting some initial gender identity pieces together.

With drips and drabs of stories about transgender slipping out of the nascent media of the era. Three network TV stations, venerable Chicago station WGN, and pre-PBS "educational" station WTTW, the *Chicago Tribune*, and the *Sun-Times*, occasionally published stories about people having a "sex change."

Although other people giggled at the thought, I was thinking, "Can people really do that?" I researched the topic as well as I could at the town library, pulling out medical books and devouring everything I could find about transvestites, transgender, transsexual, and sex changes, while hiding in the stacks from any proper town librarian, who might discover what I was reading and bust me.

It was frightening reading about these topics, as I was obviously fighting a deep and conflicting inner sense of my own identity, while at the same time feeling a distance from it all, as I was in deep denial that this was or could possibly be me. I thought about this intensely most of my whole life, but I always retreated into denial, fearing this could not actually be me. It must be something else. At that point in my life, I lived with constant inner turmoil and confusion.

This confirmation of what I was becoming began a worsening secret world of shame and confusion, pain and hiding. At the same time, as my conventional female friends' bodies developed, I always thought, "Why can't mine just develop more fully like theirs?" Clearly a difficult time for me.

12. Suicidal Ideation

In junior high school, after a lifetime of repressing my gender-conflicted feelings, the dissonance between my mind, body, and life itself increasingly became too much to handle. Every morning, I woke up feeling more shame, confusion, and anxiety than the day before, yet had to hide my thoughts from everyone I knew. I was sometimes fearful that they could actually hear my thoughts.

I started to fantasize about how to kill myself. But I think I was saved from this by a tragic event. One night, a friend's father walked in front of an oncoming speeding commuter train in our serene suburban town. Unfortunately, I happened to see part of his remains in a tree the next day. That vivid graphic event was enough to quickly end my thoughts about suicide. (Besides, I faint at the sight of blood.)

By that point in my life, I was thinking most of the time as a woman and becoming a woman, and was starting to transform into the person I was to become, discovering an inner, albeit secretive, peace.

Separately, I was also discovering myself in other areas such as writing and music, the culture and mood of the times, the growing tumultuous politics of the era, while generally coming to a first-time sense of understanding of who I really was. That inner sense of joy and contentment has held me together ever since.

13. College Days & Earth Shoes

My college years coincided with the height of the Vietnam War, and all bets were off in terms of society being able to tell us what should be and what was. With old people defined as those over 30, whom could you trust? We now had the military/industrial complex to deal with—and increasingly, living in a world seeing friends going off to an unjust war. These events were seen for the first time in color on TV in our homes, and some friends were never to come home again. A powerful sense of questioning, exploration, discovery, revolt, and freedom on all fronts was the norm of the era.

Peace. Purple Haze. Woodstock. Free love. Sex. Tie-dye. Earth Shoes. *Mother Earth News. The Whole Earth Catalog.* Granola. Bra-burning (I had many by then, and now wish I had kept them)! All done in the communal spirit of our brethren students —from Berkeley to Boston—to end an unjust war. I took up the drug of choice for the era (*Giggle Weed. Green Goddess. Mary Jane. Reefer*), albeit for just one year.

But after an ethereal year of fog, smoke, and haze squandered away, I realized I had missed a solid year of college, at least on the weekends and on any coherent and cognitive level. I found I was doing things I really didn't need help with, like eating an entire bag of OREO Double Stuf cookies, and not being able to remember key words—like my name. So, it was cold turkey (and a little gravy on the side) from that year on. After a year of the giggles, those were the last of my hallucinatory days.

Despite a year of euphoria, my gender dysphoria persisted. Initially, I was a music major and was heavily involved with music performance (clarinet, flute, and sax) and composition. I later switched to journalism, but have kept up music performance and composing ever since.

It was about that time that one of my favorite composers, noted *Switched-on Bach* musician Walter Carlos, transitioned to become Wendy Carlos. I had seen a quote by her saying, "I was about five or six...I remember being convinced I was a little girl, much preferring long hair and girls' clothes, and not knowing why my parents didn't see it clearly." This lingered intensely in my mind in that I knew I had the exact same feelings.

Although this mental frontline battle was constantly going on in my head, at least externally, I led and presented a relatively happy life, had many friends, and was very actively involved with school, music, ski trips, tennis, cycling, and everything else common to a typical busy college environment. I enjoyed those days immensely, at least on the outside.

I came out about my conflicting sense of gender to many of my college friends, pouring my heart out reticently, but also in a burst of joy, like a field of sunflowers dotting the Kansas plains (where I went to school), doing the best I could to hide the toll that ignoring this my whole life had taken on me.

Surprisingly, my friends were totally understanding and accepting when I was going from a male exterior—through stages of androgyny—(besides, Earth Shoes were gender-neutral) and on the journey to womanhood. It was at college that I first met other trans people and others along the complex cisgender/sexuality/gender-fluid anatomical spectrum.

It also was where I started to realize for the first time that I was hardly alone on my gender journey, which had clearly begun.

14. Love

People ask if I was ever in love. Yes. One woman. I first met her when we were much younger. Beautiful. Intelligent. Natural. Organic. Gentle. Kind. Introspective. Spiritual. Cosmic. Talented. Funny. Cute. Sexy. Dog lover. She's always been part of my life in one way or another. Mentally, emotionally, physically, and spiritually. We dated. We've been lovers. We are friends.

I think that when you fall in love with someone, well, you simply fall in love. It's quite inexplicable. It's a powerful notion. I was fortunate to meet her early in my life. We did many things together. Hiked. Canoed. Sailed. Traveled. Yoga. Music. Walked long distances. Shared books. Dieted. Drank wine. Ate cheese. Dieted some more. Spent time together at our lake.

I've had many wonderful girlfriends, but how can you think about them, at least on a deep emotional level, when you really care about just one woman?

We've both gone through a lot since we first met. Triumphs and joys, illness and healing, loss and growth, spouses, divorce, and change. She will always hold a special and sole place in my heart. I still love her very much. I will always love her.

15. Becoming a Woman

After college and into adulthood, I was still living primarily as a male, at least on the outside. But with strong societal expectations etched into my brain, I attempted to "be a man" by doing what was considered to be "manly" things—playing and watching sports and "bellying up to the bar" to talk about sports and about women, often inappropriately and uncomfortably. My attempts to be "macho," however, were difficult and more like a caricature than what an actual man should be. I kept up the "guy" act as well as I could, at least partially, when I was young.

Eventually, I realized I couldn't continue to deny who I was. I was in deep turmoil, wracked with guilt and shame, and in a constant state of denial, naively thinking this would all just go away. I struggled excruciatingly for many years with whom I was becoming. This was after many years of intense, repressed, internal conflict, during which I experienced stomach ulcers, GERD, anxiety, and depression. I was prescribed various antidepressants and talk therapy—always secretly—due to a deep fear of being exposed.

16. Marriage and Friends

I married in my late 20s. I was lucky to find a wonderful woman after my college years. Very positive and even-keeled. Solid. Strong. Organized. Originally from near Normal, Illinois. (Yes, there is really a city named "Normal") I like to say I married a "normal" woman.

She was a good wife and is an incredible mother—very smart, clearly the source of my intellectually-gifted children. Today, she works at an Ivy League university in a profession she is very good at.

Another part of this story: I was married a second time to another woman, albeit very briefly. It was a traumatic time and a dark period in my life. It is extremely difficult to write about, but certainly part of my journey—as painful as it was.

At that point in my life, I had been living as a woman. She knew and accepted that, I believe appreciating me as much as a girlfriend as a male friend. She was very beautiful, very feminine. I later learned through intensive counseling that I was likely attracted to her "china doll" traits. In some ways, at least initially, it was an amazing relationship: free, fun, spontaneous, and chaotic. She was a partner who could accept me as who I really was.

What I did not know is that she had the symptoms of borderline personality disorder (BPD), a serious mental illness characterized by pervasive instability of moods, interpersonal relationships, self-image, and behavior. It's way beyond the scope of this book to discuss this disorder in depth. However, this instability often disrupts family and work life, long-term planning, and an individual's sense of identity.

I was living on the edge in constant fear. Sometimes in the protection of a neighbor, friend, or local police. I have no malice or blame toward her, as I obviously was attracted to her, but the words "living nightmare" would hardly describe the anger, rage, and often violence I regularly experienced.

It was impossible to focus on my gender identity while managing the intense, pervasive fear. Although the total relationship lasted less than two years, it was fraught with drama, trauma, and constant terror. I had to move into a separate, locked bedroom and keep knives under my bed.

The relationship included significant incidents, such as the destruction of our home and belongings, hoarding, attempts to run me over with a car, a wine bottle cracked on my skull, scalding hot coffee thrown in my face, and finally, an attempt to stab me with a butter knife, among other acts of violence. (Later, I told the court that if I'm going to be killed with a knife, it had better be a meat cleaver and be done with it! Death by butter knife is a bad way to go.) All these actions led to several restraining orders and eventually, divorce.

I still view this as a bizarre anomaly in my life that I will never fully understand, but it certainly was part of my life journey, and one I know I will never repeat. How my gender was impacted, I'm not quite sure, but after that marriage ended, I became a woman in all ways.

It was only after some twenty years of a very conventional and happy marriage and the raising of two amazing daughters in Illinois, Arizona, and Connecticut, then later in New Jersey, that I eventually became myself. But even at that point, I could think of little else than my desire to be a woman.

In those days, like many others, I regularly "dressed" privately or secretly at any opportunity I could, usually as part of business travel in other cities, increasingly taking more steps of transition. I was meeting and connecting with other trans woman on the East Coast, taking courses at Columbia University's gender study program, and regularly attending support groups through Tri-Ess, the international transgender sorority.

I remember once at a "girls' night out" dinner in White Plaines, New York, a town far from mine to prevent any exposure, meeting a very nice and sweet girl sitting next to me. Girls are usually loath to talk much about their other "self" in such settings for many reasons. But this woman shared with me the town she lived in as her male persona, and it turned out to be the same as mine, Darien, Connecticut, about 20 miles away and safely across state lines. She was the high school football coach in a very conservative, sports-crazed suburban town. So, it was amazing for me to see "him" at our Saturday football games!

Most of my transition in those days were secretive, guilt-ridden, and generally difficult. I remember one time very early on, while working in Richmond, Virginia, a city in which I spent a lot of time on assignment over many years, was one of the first times I dared to venture out as a female.

I had just bought some clothes at a woman's clothing store I regularly frequented, but I was in the habit of changing back to a male to go outside. But my retail friend asked why I did that, conveying that I looked fine. So, out the door I went—for the first time dressed as a woman.

I was terrified. With great trepidation, I stepped onto the busy sidewalk, for some reason thinking the entire city would stop and point at me and "out" me. But no. Nothing. No one even looked at me. So, in amazement with my new status, I boldly walked into a mall, blended in, and started shopping. And have never looked back. I now had considerable confidence for the first time that I could live the life I wanted, and be the person I was becoming.

Like many, but not all, transgender women, my inner being indirectly led to divorce. Although there were other issues, being trans would not likely be accepted in my marriage, even though there was a modicum of knowledge that I was transgender. However, I don't think she or I comprehended the depth of what being transgender is all about. Although I know many happily married trans couples at all points on the gender spectrum, this would not likely have worked for her.

I've been lucky, however, to have dozens of very close friends I met through my work, school, and life in one way or another, friends I'm still as close with today as the day we met.

17. Work

Like most people, my life was and is shaped significantly by work. By a career. An identity. But since the focus of this book is on my gender identity, I don't write specifically here about my work. However, for the record, my career has been and is about communications, writing, journalism, radio, TV, film, public relations, and music in one way or another, primarily in Chicago and New York. However, gender identity has always been underneath or integrally part of it as well.

It was always there, but not until my external "transition" did it become evident and communicated to others. In terms of process and timing, early on, I always lived and dressed as a woman wherever I could, e.g., travel, meetings, parties, at hotels, and anywhere else it seemed appropriate.

I had also found that dressing as a woman created a centering feeling of peace, allowing me to be my inner self, essentially providing a sense of comfort and normalcy during the intense pressures of work. (I've always said that

Off to work.

working in Midtown Manhattan in Big Time PR is not for the faint of heart.) However, my inner conflict deepened as I maintained this deep, dark secret inside, constantly fearing I would be discovered.

I've worked primarily in public relations, evolving to senior-level positions in large New York PR firms and at two Fortune 500 companies. Part of my job has always been working with celebrities on media tours, concerts, events, promotions, ads, PSAs (public service announcements), media training, spokespersons, award banquets, galas, and so on, which to the uninitiated, tends to portray a sense or glamour to the work. Regardless, since this is part of the job, celebrities like to be treated professionally and with respect, so it becomes remarkably part and parcel of the job.

Most celebrities have been very easy to work with. And some who stand out and with whom I have had the opportunity to work, and often continued to maintain a relationship with include Terry Bradshaw, Ken Burns, Dick Button, Chick Corea, Katie Couric, Eddie Gomez (jazz bass player), Marvin Hamlisch, Bob Hope, Al Jarreau, Robert Joffrey, Michael Jordan, Garrison Keillor, Hubert Laws, Arnold Palmer, Marian McPartland, Rod Serling, Ravi Shankar, Joe Torre, and Eudora Welty (renowned Southern writer), among others.

During the early part of my career, I nevertheless had to keep my gender identity hidden, since transgender people faced—and continue to face—significant discrimination in the workplace, where rampant and chronic bias and unemployment are pervasive. If your presentation does not rigidly conform to the gender binary, you will likely be harassed on all levels.

It is ironic that I knew many trans people in the workplace, but did not have the courage to come out myself, since I had seen firsthand the implicit and direct discrimination that occurred. For example, once, when working in New York, I was asked to find "dirt" on a talented web designer in our Florida office to ultimately terminate him. This was horrible for me. It would be generous to say that I heard senior management say discriminatory, marginalizing, and outright hurtful and hateful words about this person, joking with me about this "perverted" person, while they asked me to participate from an "objective" perspective in the witch-hunt cabal (I ran the New York office at that time) when of course, the irony was that I was trans myself!

After a lot of angst and thought, I decided to work with the other senior managers to try to find a way to let Michael—now Michelle—transition and keep her job, which she ultimately did. I didn't have to "out" myself in the process. No one ever knew I was transgender, but I'm sure Michelle suspected I was; and I know she appreciated my support of her.

As I continued to go down the dual paths of career and my secret and evolving gender identity, I felt the severe consequences of these two worlds colliding.

Society demands that you submerge your true identity and act out to be the person society expects you to be. It forces

Getting a smooch from Al Jarreau (2015)

The author and legendary jazz double
bassist, Eddie Gomez
(Photograph by Amy Wilbourne, 2018)

you to constantly pretend you are a man so that you would be rewarded with success and recognition (and higher pay). All the while, you know that if you got "caught," it would be the end of your position in the workforce, status in society, and certainly your career.

It was also difficult to function, as I was plagued with self-doubt, guilt, depression, and anxiety—sometimes wondering why I should work so hard if I didn't even like the forced façade of the life I was living, always knowing that if I were to come out as transgender, I would be banished to a life of an outcast. I knew that something had to change because I couldn't go on living such a tormented life as the dissonance grew deeper and wider.

As I transitioned, I started my own communications firm, CarlaAnne Communications, that primarily provides services for Fortune 500 companies, focusing particularly on employee engagement and internal communications, and of course, allows me to be myself. I also have an online retail women's apparel company called SeriousShapewear—Contours for the discriminating Woman (http://www.seriousshapewear.com) and The Writers' Block (http://thewritersblock.info), a consortium of top-tier writers for companies that need great copy. Separately, I also write music for film and television and perform as a woodwind instrumentalist (clarinet, flute, and sax), primarily classical and jazz music in a variety of ensembles.

On a more positive note, as I started to slowly evolve and transition, a huge burden was lifted off my psyche as I discovered a new, unbounding sense of strength, zest for life, and inner joy. The more I became authentic and true to myself, the more I found renewed interest and strengths I never knew I had. With a deep sense of happiness melding in my work and personal life, it's difficult to convey in words the profound sense of peace and solace that these changes brought to my emotional, mental, and physical states.

18. Intolerance, Discrimination & Hate

Being a generally very positive and happy person, I hesitate to emit negativity into the Universe. But since intolerance, discrimination, and hate are unfortunately so much part of the transgender experience, I feel compelled to share at least three setbacks in my life, mostly as a progenitor to help others avoid what happened to me.

One incident was the time I was brutally beaten and mugged by four youths. I later learned, through subsequent court hearings, that the attack was that the assailants suspected me of being transgender. Sparing the gory details, essentially, I was walking out of a restaurant early on a very cold Friday night. They had seen me in the restaurant, and while I was in the ladies' room preparing to leave, they waited for me outside the restaurant.

As I walked outside, I felt a very hard thud on the back of my head, which turned out to be the handle of a gun, knocking me to the ground, where they jumped on me, washed my face with ice and stones, spit in my face, kicked me in the groin, said disparaging words, and hit me again on the head as I tried to lift my head up to see who they were.

It dropped back down into a dripping pool of blood from my cracked skull. Then they ran off with my purse and laptop. Thankfully, my prone and damaged body was discovered within minutes, the police and ambulance arrived, I spent the night in ER, and began a long physical and psychological recovery process.

I was very fortunate. My possessions were quickly recovered since my assailants were never after them in the first place. Three of the four youths were eventually apprehended and jailed, while the fourth escaped on a bus to Indiana. (Hey, what's worse, living in the culturally enriched, hip, and vibrant City of Milwaukee, or the plains of Indiana?)

Under the heading of "stupid criminals," by taking and using my Mac laptop and iPhone, the devices immediately sent a signal to a satellite, back down to Earth, and directly to the detectives with very specific GPS coordinates saying, "Here's where we are. Here's the shortest route in traffic. Please come and get us!" (Thanks, Apple!)

To assure they would get found, the entire incident was recorded on security cameras. The court case later revealed their actions were a hate crime. People do get mugged, but this certainly was a very scary incident, very real, and an example of what transgender people have to contend with all over the world and need to be cognizant about. I feel lucky it was not much worse.

Another time, less physically violent if not emotionally distressing, when stopping at a combined gas station, gun and ammo store in the town near our summer cottage owned by a long-time legacy family in the region, a place we frequented for three generations, it became apparent to the owners that I was the same person they had known growing up in the area, but as a young boy.

That particular day when I stopped for gas, the couple who owned the store pulled me aside and asked me to step into their back office. It was a room adorned with guns, ammunition, prepper survival kits, a wall of trophy animal heads, and one book in the center of the room, yes, the Good Book. They asked me if I had thought about my soul. I said yes, but I don't think that was the answer they were looking for.

Reminiscent of the scene in *Midnight Cowboy* when Joe Buck is trapped by a seedy, street-corner-styled evangelist in a westside hotel who plugs in a hollow, tinted plastic Jesus statue that glows on the dresser, then tells Joe Buck to "get down on our knees, now"—in that back room, the gas station owners told me to start praying for my soul, and for the next hour or two, proselytized me and read me Bible verses.

I tried to convey that I was a Christian (albeit a transgender one) and believed I was loved by God regardless, but I could see my entreaty was landing on deaf ears. I finally convinced them to let me go, but not without them telling me I should "change my immoral ways!" If I didn't, they said, if they saw me any-where in the area, they made it clear that they would have me "accommodated" by one of their friends. (It always gets my attention when told that by people who sell guns.)

Well, the good news is, I still go to the town for all my needs and haven't yet been "accommodated." I even attend the small church in the town where I have many wonderful friends. I plan to continue being part of the town, but I think that may not be a good store for me to get my gas. Or guns. Or ammo. (It's OK. I don't hunt.)

A third setback, perhaps the most distressing and painful of them all, was an incident with a family member who has always had great difficulty in understanding what I had gone through and who I am, and certainly in trying to accept the fact that I am transgender. After years of general hostility, he suggested we meet for breakfast one cold, snowy Saturday morning at Christmas time in Milwaukee, about two hours from where he lives.

I felt that perhaps the messages of joy, love, and acceptance associated with the season had softened his feelings and vitriolic harangues after all these years. I had not seen him for many years, and certainly not as myself. Although I was enthused about the rendezvous, I was also reticent and nervous, and had prepared in my mind words along the lines of, "I know this is difficult for you. I appreciate us convening, and would be happy to talk about who I am and what this is all about."

Well, our encounter did not go that way. He arrived at the designated restaurant. I was dressed in a conservative outfit appropriate for a church meeting scheduled later that day. As soon as he saw me, however, he said in a curt voice, "I can't condone the decision you made. You need to get professional help, and I don't want you to ever present yourself to our family that way." He then turned around, walked out, and drove back home in the blizzard.

I felt like I had been slugged in my stomach. Words like "devastated" hardly convey my emotional state. I sat down, unable to move for the next two hours or do anything other than sip my coffee, while trying to explain to the chirpy waitress with tears in my eyes that something came up and he had to go and we were not going to eat. So, that went well.

I've always felt lucky that my transition was not as painful as that of many others who have gone through what I've experienced. Although I had at least surmised that living an authentic life would not be easy, the hardest part is understanding from where the hate is coming. Simply not knowing why.

So why do so many people hate transgender people and act violently towards them? I don't know but would conjecture that it's easy for people to hate those whom they don't understand. Like all other prejudices, transphobia is based on misconceptions and negative stereotypes that are used to "justify" discrimination, harassment, and even hate crimes. It's similar to racism, sexism, and marginalization against people with disabilities.

Transphobia consists of a range of adverse attitudes, feelings, or actions toward transgender persons. It manifests itself in discomfort, fear, anger, or violence. Often expressed alongside homophobic views, transphobia is often considered an aspect of homophobia. Some people hate transgender people because they think that we are perverts, rapists, or are intentionally acting against what is morally right. Some from believing that those that identify as transgender is a choice.

I live in a world where transgender people not only face discrimination, but are shot, dismembered, mutilated, stabbed, strangled, hanged, burned, and beaten to death. I've been lucky that I have not been a victim to that extent. Although physical violence is no picnic, I've found that the psychological impact of hate can be even worse. For me, being showered with hatred and marginalization is like being stabbed in the stomach with a knife.

19. Trans Connections

Once Al Gore "invented" the Internet, I learned that I was hardly alone in my gender identity challenges. I started meeting dozens of trans people online and convening regularly in person for all kinds of trans activities, socials, educational, political, and other related events.

By that time—I think around my early 30s—I also had a heightened awareness of trans people all around me, and eventually had the courage to speak to them as I identified increasingly with them, as they did with me, when I was dressed and out and about as a woman. I also started taking courses centered on gender transition at Columbia University's Institute for Research on Women, Gender, and Sexuality in New York City, and speaking with many groups in that supportive setting.

All this seemed very strange at first, meeting so many trans people, where on one level I felt I was not really part of this strange new world. Yet at the same time, I knew it was increasingly becoming my world in a very deep and profound way. Now I was regularly connecting with hundreds of transgender people online from all over the country, often meeting them, albeit still stealthily, in the New York City area and at other places I regularly traveled to on business.

20. The End of Pretending

"Because I am me, just as you are you. We don't always
get to pick who we are, but we can choose to celebrate it."
—Nathan Reese Maher, author

On one level, I had hoped for most of my life that my gender dysphoria would simply go away. That it would be something I could fix. Outgrow. That by trying to act like "one of the guys," this would distract me from my true inner sense of being.

But of course, being transgender never goes away. It only intensifies. You find yourself thinking, "Why can't I be comfortable in my own skin like every other man or woman?" You wish that you could wake up just one morning and not have this gender thing always confronting you.

For me, I did not become a woman; I simply stopped pretending to be a man. For my journey, most of my life I have lived very happily, at least externally. However, I don't feel I actually transitioned at all since it was the only existence I knew. And for the last 20 years or so, I've lived fully as a woman—inwardly, mentally, emotionally, physically, outwardly, joyfully, peacefully, and legally; and increasingly if not totally, openly to everyone I've ever known if they wanted to know or even cared.

Today, I have nothing to hide, nothing to lie about. I see myself as a woman simply because I am a woman. It is my gender. It is who I am. Rather, it's profoundly integral to my inner sense of being. What's odd to me is that this is so much my inner and external sense of being that I forget that I've ever been anything else, I guess because this is who I have always been.

SECTION THREE

Transgender in a Non-Transgender World

"We don't want anything other than our humanity,"
—Jennifer Finney Boylan

1. An Historical Perspective

Throughout time, all cultures have experienced transgender people and have recognized them in different ways. Whatever culture, country, or epoch you explore—from ancient Greek and Roman writings to modern-day, multicultural societies—you will find a history and breadth of individuals who are viewed as being transgender.

For example, indigenous North Americans used the term "two spirit" to describe certain spiritual people in their communities who identify as both male and female, and/or who fulfill a traditional third-gender (or other gender-variant) role in their cultures. In more than 150 American tribes, "two spirit" is seen as having a special and elevated role, where gender ambiguity is not only fully accepted, but actually revered as one with both a masculine and feminine perspective, offering greater wisdom.

That said, society, particularly Western culture, can be very harsh on gender-variant people. This has resulted in many transgender people losing their families, friends, jobs, homes, support, and even their lives. Western culture tends to be "genitally" obsessed when it comes to gender. Body form and plumbing are often what our society sees. What's between one's legs and on one's chest impacts sex and reproduction, not gender. It does not necessarily determine one's sexual orientation or ability to have a healthy and happy sexual relationship.

This further illustrates the need to understand gender as a complex, three-dimensional matrix of male/female expression on a shifting spectrum, not as an either/or classification based simply on the appearance of physical genitalia. Thus, there's a significant need for society to understand the true individual who is long buried under the layers of society's artificially imposed expectations and judgments.

2. In the News

Today, one can't search the news without finding several daily stories about transgender, transgender people, and gender transition. Like anyone else, transgender people make news of all kinds, and every day, there are dozens of transgender stories in the media. The good news is that the media is increasingly treating trans stories more intelligently and with more balance and insight, less sensationally and with a higher sense of enlightenment. That said, unfortunately, many stories still are horrific about beatings, harassment, suicides, and sometimes killings.

With the year 2014 being called by *TIME* magazine the "Year of Transgender," the mainstream media increasingly cover transgender more intelligently. I'm comforted to see increasing levels of respectful coverage, understanding, and support, particularly helping to convey to the non-trans world what transgender is actually about.

We are starting to see some level of societal understanding and acceptance of transgender people as human beings with dignity, thus encouraging the media to develop stories that are more thoroughly covered, less judgmental, and with more accuracy. They present transgender people from all walks of life, professions, cultures, countries, ages, and from throughout history.

3. In Music

Even as I write this book, there's a story on the radio in the background about lead rock 'n' roll singer Laura Jane Grace who recently transitioned and released her current album conveying her feelings of gender dysphoria, front and center.

Laura Jane Grace

I share this because it's playing in the background as I write, but like so many of these kinds of stories, I can totally relate to her feelings. In her case, when asked what it was like to release her first album as a woman, she said it was "completely freeing and liberating." When asked when she first felt she was in the wrong body, she said, "My earliest memories are of dysphoria. I vividly remember . . . I was probably about four years old and lived in Texas at the time. There was a Madonna concert on TV and I just remember feeling self-recognition: 'That's me, and that's what I want to do. Just be myself.'"

Laura Jane was then asked how, after suppressing these feelings for her whole life, her transition made her feel. She said, "It's a frightening feeling since there's so much uncertainty, as if you've made a decision, even though it wasn't really a decision at all, because it was based on, 'Either I'm going to kill myself, or I need to address this.' I don't have a map going forward. I don't have all the answers. I know this is something that's going to potentially cause a lot of uncertainty for things I don't want to change, but all I know is that I'm completely happy."

She concluded, "I'm willing to talk about this stuff and am happy to do interviews since I accept the fact that many have questions because transgender is something new to many people. But I know it's not what's is really important. For me, the key to my happiness is to be making sure you write great songs and put on great shows. That's all that actually matters."

I can relate.

4. In the Media

Increasingly, more thoughtful writing is becoming typical of long -lead media, such as magazines, books, and film about transgender. Another story, also in today's news, is about the successful American author, journalist, magazine editor, and talk -show host Janet Mock and her insightful book, *Redefining Realness, My Path to Womanhood, Identity, Love & So Much More*.

Mock talks about coming of age as a trans woman in Hawaii. Her advice to media: "View trans people as people." She adds, "There's a layer of deep-seated internalized dehumanization of trans people and their bodies. That creates a kind of separation between the journalist and the trans person they're speaking to. This separation would never happen if they didn't know the person was trans. For example, you wouldn't ask a traditional woman about her genitals...because we're trans, our bodies are not open for inspection."

I can relate.

Drucker & Ernst

Another notable "trans-news" item, again just as I write, is an interesting opening of a photo series for the Whitney Museum of Art Biennial called *Relationship* by media artists Rhys Ernst and Zackary Drucker: http://whitney.org/Exhibitions/2014Biennial/ZackaryDruckerAndRhysErnst

Ernst (no relation) is transitioning from female to male, while Drucker is transitioning from male to female. The exhibit photos detail their developing relationship and their transitioning bodies as each traverse the gender spectrum.

Drucker: "The amazing thing about being a human is that we're transformative material and we change from one moment to the next. Being transgender is a more visible manifestation of that because we're literally changing the way we are presenting ourselves to the world."

Ernst: "When we met and fell in love, our experience really transcended ideas about finite categories of sexual preference and identity, and gender identity, and it sort of just collapsed all that into meaningless boxes. I believe that there is something, hopefully, very powerful about that, that other people can relate to."

I can relate.

More can be read about Drucker and Ernst in a follow-up 2014 *New York Times* article by Jacob Bernstein: "In Their Own Terms—The Growing Transgender Presence in Pop Culture" www.nytimes.com/2014/03/13/fashion/the-growing-transgender-presence-in-pop-culture.html?_r=0

Laverne Cox

Recently, *Orange is the New Black* star Laverne Cox appeared on the cover of *TIME* magazine with the headline "The Transgender Tipping Point." (http://time.com/135480/transgender-tipping-point/.) However, unfortunately, after those years of "trans-enlightenment," the societal pendulum tipped the other direction, expressed eloquently by Samantha Allen of *The Daily Beast* in her article "After the optimism of 2014, conveying how "after the 'Transgender Tipping Point" as decreed by *TIME,* trans people are now facing an onslaught of legislative prejudice."

5. On TV

With the transgender world becoming increasingly visible, television has only begun to reflect those changes in a variety of programs—ranging from topics about transgender, and slowly seeing transgender people being assimilated into the stories. It's difficult to miss what's a shift towards increased understanding, acceptance, and positive coverage of transgender by mainstream media.

Transparent is the powerful and funny story by Jill Soloway about a clan of secular LA Jews, where the father, a long-divorced former professor named "Mort" (Jeffrey Tambor), who in retirement begins his M2F transition and coming out as "Maura Pfefferman."

As *New Yorker* reviewer Emily Nussbaum so adroitly said, "By Soloway's conveying Maura as a mirror, reflecting back the 'queerness' in everyone around her, she's free to critique a certain generational strain of urbane self-obsession, one that merges self-love with self-loathing." This makes the show extraordinary on many levels, way beyond the transgender component. Tambor won an Emmy in 2015 and again in 2016 for Outstanding Actor in a Comedy Series, and in his acceptance speech, a visibly touched Tambor noted, "This is big. This is much bigger than me. I would like to dedicate my performance and this award to the transgender community. Thank you for your inspiration, thank you for your patience, and thank you for letting us be a part of the change."

For me, it's interesting and a bit overwhelming to see the public beginning to embrace a television program dealing with transgender openly, positively, and powerfully.

In the much older genre of theater, "gender bending" as a theme has been around since ancient Greece. For example, Shakespeare's *Twelfth Night* in the 1600s, a play about many topics, including gender fluidity, foreshadows many of today's transgender issues in a surprisingly resonant manner. Viola's masculine strength and Cesario's feminine sensitivity add to the romantic confusion as the playful gender-bending story explores the many incarnations love can take. The play shows that you can fall in love with the essence of a person—the person's spirit and soul—not necessarily the individual's gender.

Chaz Bono
Other visible trans people in the media include transman Chaz Bono, the American advocate, writer, musician, actor, and child of entertainers Sonny and Cher.

Chelsea Manning
She is the controversial transwoman and U.S. Army soldier convicted for leaking Army secrets and later released.

ABC Family Network's *Becoming Us*
Historically, at the forefront of showcasing the changing model of family in America, ABC Family Network's transgender reality show *Becoming Us* debuted in June of 2015. This show is about

two typical Midwestern teenagers (who are dating), while both their fathers are transitioning into women.

On one show, Danielle's trans parent says, "I wouldn't wish a gender conflict upon anybody. It's a nightmare, it's not a hobby, it's reality." And Ben Lehwald's parent, Carly Lehwald, says, "It's not easy. There's so much to it. Being completely re-socialized is just so huge. Finding out what it's like to be stared at. Pointed at, snickered at, laughed at. It's pretty intense. There are many aspects that are really difficult. But at the same time, there's also just so much freedom and joy that comes with it. Not necessarily being transgender, but knowing who you are and living who you are."

Gender Revolution – A Journey with Katie Couric

There have been many documentaries and feature films about transgender over the years—too many to enumerate here—but my observation is that the tone has changed from transgender being some sort of rare and misunderstood oddity, to more substantive and better balanced reporting, and increasingly on traditional media.

Notably, there was a special issue of *National Geographic* magazine that delves into the evolving topic of gender identity and its shifting landscape called "Gender Revolution" and a compatible two-hour special on the National Geographic Society Channel entitled *Gender Revolution – A Journey with Katie Couric* (http://channel.nationalgeographic.com/gender-revolution-a-journey-with-katie-couric/videos/gender-revolution-a-journey-with-katie-couric2).

The feature article and film particularly focus on science as a way to help people better understand and navigate the complex world of gender identity, and the film explores the intricacies of gender in everyday life, from the moment of birth through the twilight years. Couric examines the evolving world of transgender and all its complexities with scientists, activists, transgender people, and parents of intersex and transgender children. From college students to married couples, Couric says "It's a story of personal journey and the science ... I don't think we ever truly get to know the individuals who are really having an impact on public policy."

A particularly enlightened response to the film and transgender in general is well conveyed in an interview with Katie Couric by Ellen DeGeneres at youtube.com/watch?v=us-ks7Z23NY, and among many interesting comments made, Ellen said, "Just because I'm gay, doesn't mean I know much about the world of transgender . . . people who have a different gender in their head, it's a biological, real thing." I think this shows that how misunderstood transgender is to all groups, including all the other members of the LGBTQ community.

Andreja Pejić

In the fashion world, Australian model Andreja Pejic made history by becoming the first transgender woman to be profiled in Vogue. Before completing her transition into womanhood in late 2013, Pejić was known as the first completely androgynous supermodel. Today, she's one of the most recognizable transgender models in the world.

6. In Books

Jennifer Finney Boylan

In the book arena, noted American author and political activist Jennifer Finney Boylan wrote her 2003 autobiography *She's Not There: A Life in Two Genders*, the first book by an openly transgender American to become a bestseller. She is on the faculty of Barnard College of Columbia University. She has two sons, Zach and Sean, with Deirdre Boylan, whom she married in 1988 as James Boylan.

Today, the couple is still married and residing between New York City and Belgrade Lakes, Maine. Nine years after she began her transition, Boylan published an article for the *New York Times* conveying, "My spouse and I love each other. Our legal union has been a good thing—for us, for our children, and for our community."

Janet Mock

Janet Mock is an American writer, TV host, transgender rights activist, author of the *New York Times* bestseller *Redefining Realness*, contributing editor for *Marie Claire*, and former staff editor of *People* magazine's website. Mock lives in New York City with her husband, photographer Aaron Tredwell.

Writers like Boylan and Mock are just some of the many transgender and non-transgender individuals who are shaping the national discussion about transgender culture, human rights, and advocacy.

Amy Ellis Nutt

In her recent book, *Becoming Nicole: The Transformation of an American Family*, Pulitzer Prize-winning journalist Amy Ellis Nutt tells the honest, intimate story about two adopted identical twin boys named Jonas and Wyatt Maines, and how Wyatt became Nicole. This account reveals how their mother Kelly's certainty that she would do whatever it took to raise happy children overcame her fears, and how their father Wayne struggled to accept what identical twin brother Jonas always knew.

The author discussed many interesting points on a recent NPR interview. One was regarding the DSM [Diagnostic and Statistical Manual of Mental Disorders] that changed "gender identity disorder" to "gender identity dysphoria" in 2013, and the significance of that change.

She said, "I think the most important thing is that it changes the view of gender identity, or of an anomalous gender identity, as being somehow abnormal. It's not a disorder. The problem for kids—and all for transgender people—isn't within, it's without. In other words, their trouble with their gender identity comes essentially because others view them one way, when they view themselves another.

Nicole, for instance, knew that she was a girl, but she also knew that people referred to her as a boy and that she had a boy's anatomy. This was a child who was never unsure of who she was, but she knew there was a problem with how other people and the rest of the world viewed her. And that's where the dysphoria comes in—when there's a mismatch between what we expect and what, perhaps, the sexual anatomy says, and what the brain is telling us."

Regarding the fluidity of gender, Nutt says, "Gender isn't something that's necessarily fixed; it's dynamic, it's fluid . . . There are very few people who are 100 percent totally masculine or 100 percent totally feminine. We have traits of both, and so, ordinarily, it's something in between. I think people are feeling more comfortable now saying, 'Yeah, I've never felt 100 percent masculine, but I'm mostly masculine.' And, I think, it has become a more comfortable society to say that in. But it's also because people see how the science supports that."

I first heard a moving and enlightening interview with Nichole Maines on NPR's Terry Gross's Fresh Air at: https://www.youtube.com/watch?v=D2_wHpsEZ6g. Now a transgender activist, Maines is quite present on the media, but a particularly moving presentation of her challenging journey is conveyed at a TedTalk at www.youtube.com/watch?v=bXnTAnsVfN8.

This very moving and poignant video with Nichole Maines and her father, Wayne Maines (https://www.youtube.com/watch?v=irr7OinmKMQ), highlights Wayne's eventual acceptance of his transgender daughter Nichole. He says, "transgender children and their parents are probably some of the bravest people I have ever met." He also tearfully shares his alarm over the high rate of suicide in the transgender community, particularly for children, with a 50 percent suicide attempt rate for transgender youth from ages 10 to 25, where the average rate among the general population is two to four percent. He adds that transgender kids often "have no hope and do not want to be alive. I realized that I either had to accept who my child was, or that I might not have my baby. No kid should have to persevere like that."

Today, there are many more books on transgender, with new ones increasingly coming out (so to speak) every day, and way more than can be enumerated within this book, but a few more that are particularly informative, entertaining, and notable include:

- *I am Jazz* by Jessica Herthel
- *Gender Outlaw* by Kate Bornstein
- *Middlesex* by Jeffrey Eugenides
- *Luna* by Julie Anne Peters
- *Cobra* by Severo Sarduy
- *Stone Butch Blues* by Leslie Feinberg
- *Man Enough to be a Woman* by Jayne County
- *Sex Changes: The Politics of Transgenderism* by Patrick Califia
- *Invisible Lives: The Erasure of Transsexual and Transgendered People* by Viviane K Namaste
- *Whipping Girl: A Transsexual Woman on Sexism and the Scapegoating of Femininity* by Julia Serano
- *Transgender History* by Susan Stryker
- *Man into Woman: The First Sex Change (a portrait of Lili Elbe)* by Niels Hoyer
- *Trans: A Memoir* by Juliet Jacques

Academic institutions are increasingly removing the gender shackles. For instance, women's college Barnard College announced that it would join traditional women's colleges Wellesley, Mount Holyoke, and Smith in enrolling transgender women. Such developments suggest that transgender men and women have made strides toward acceptance.

7. At the Movies

Gender variation and fluidity has been part of film since its inception in the 1900s, albeit relegated to the sidelines in the dawn of the burgeoning new medium.

Excluding screwball comedies such as *I was a Male War Bride* in 1949, and Billy Wilder's *Some Like it Hot* in 1959, and later comedies such as *Tootsie* and *Mrs. Doubtfire*, it was not until the 1960s that transgender themes became more present as subjects of feature films and documentaries moved to the center of the story, reflecting society's understanding and acceptance of transgender.

By the 1990s, film styles increasingly reflected evolving tastes, creating a wide variety of self-aware, introspective, independent, and groundbreaking films, including many dealing with transgender. There are many films that deal with the topic—beyond the scope of this book—but some notable films include:

Paris is Burning (1990) – Jennie Livingston's documentary about African-American and Latino people of various gender identities who competed in New York's glamorous balls.

The Crying Game (1992) – Neil Jordan's high stakes British-Irish psychological thriller set to the backdrop of the Irish Troubles where the protagonist falls for a woman, but he discovers that she is transgender.

Ma vie en rose (My Life in Pink) (1997) – One of the most sensitive of a wave of 1990s trans movies, Alain Berliner's drama portrays the story of Ludovic, a child seen by family and community as a boy, but who consistently communicates being a girl, depicting Ludovic's family struggling to accept his gender expression.

Boys Don't Cry (1999) – Kimberley Pierce's film dramatizes the real-life story of Brandon Teena, a transman played by Hilary Swank who adopts a male identity and attempts to find himself and love in Nebraska but falls victim to a brutal crime perpetrated by two male acquaintances. It deals intelligently with exclusion and prejudice, asking viewers to understand the layers of difficulty imposed on its protagonist, and is an important record of trans living in a particular time and place.

All about My Mother (1999) – Pedro Almodóvar's film focuses on femininity and womanhood, with a very sustained and sensitive look at trans women's lives.

Transamerica (2005) – Duncan Tucker's film featured *Desperate Housewives* star Felicity Huffman as transsexual Bree, who goes on a road trip after getting a call from her previously unknown son Toby, 17, jailed in New York.

Laurence Anyways (2012) – Xavier Dolan's film focuses on the love between cis woman Fred (short for Frederique) and transgender woman Laurence being compared to Stanley Kubrick's late-career work. Smart and observant about the difficulties of a relationship, it portrays one partner wants to restart their life in a different gender.

Boy Meets Girl (2014) – A romantic movie about growing up transgender in a small town, featuring transsexual actor Michelle Hendley.

The Danish Girl (2015) – Tom Hooper's romantic drama is inspired by the lives of Danish painters Lili Elbe and Gerda Wegener, telling the story of Elbe, one of the first known recipients of sexual reassignment surgery.

Fantastic Woman (*Una mujer fantástica*) (2017) – Chilean director Sebastián Lelio's drama about a love story "that happens to happen to a transgender woman," starring trans actress Daniela Vega as a singer mistreated in the aftermath of her boyfriend's death.

Strong Island (2018) –Yance Ford's documentary centered on the murder of Ford's brother. Ford, a transman, became the first transgender filmmaker nominated for an Oscar.

These, along with other films, help move the needle forward on transgender understanding and acceptance among the general public. In an age in which there's still violence against the transgender community, these films feature transgender characters and actors on screen as being more than just politically correct—more importantly, they tell stories that are a matter of life and death for many people. This type of non-patronizing cinema puts audiences in the shoes of the trans community, helping to create a sense of empathy and understanding in a dramatic way as no other media can do.

8. Caitlyn

And, of course, difficult to overlook—the transgender world attracted worldwide attention when former Olympian Bruce Jenner came out as a transgender woman on ABC-TV with Diane Sawyer in the summer of 2015. This created a significant catalyst of educational, productive dialogue surrounding her transition— both supportive and critical. The program helped people get exposure to and a better understanding of what transgender is, possibly come closer to acceptance, and move to being a world wherein people can live as they believe who they are.

Jenner's interview certainly helped raise awareness about the transgender community and clearly pushed the transgender rights movement into the center of the national dialogue. The highly rated interview was notable in that interviewer Diane Sawyer did not fixate on genitalia, surgery questions, sexual orientation, nor sensationalize the program with inappropriate photos or personally invasive questions. Rather, she let Jenner speak for herself.

I do think the interview helped provide further clarity about transgender issues in a very thoughtful, sensitive, and genuine way, particularly about issues such as gender vs. sexuality, shedding some light on how they have little to do with each other—a confusing area for those less exposed to the topic.

When Jenner, now as Caitlyn, was photographed shortly afterwards for *Vanity Fair* and viewed by some 46 million people, she spoke emotionally about her gender journey: "If I was lying on my deathbed and I had kept this secret and never ever did anything about it, I would be lying there saying, 'You just blew your entire life."

The Today Show

Post-media coverage, generally supportive, exploded immediately afterward, e.g., NBC's *Today Show – In Post-Caitlyn World, More Acceptance of Transgender People Expected* (http://www.nbc-news.com/news/us-news/post-jenner-world-more-acceptance-transgender-people-expected-survey-n371831). The program points out that "Caitlyn Jenner's transition is being viewed as a watershed moment for the transgender community...she's created a teachable moment for the country, and for our families ... she has given us a blueprint for compassion and acceptance ... this is not so much about her outward appearance, but her honesty."

President Barack Obama

There was an outpouring of reactions throughout the country and the world. Even the U.S. President made a comment, "All you have to do is to look at this month's cover of *Vanity Fair* to see how America is more accepting of people for who they truly are."

A considerable amount has already been written about this watershed moment with Bruce—now Caitlyn. But as time passes, it will be interesting to see how both the trans community and non-trans world ultimately view this interview and highly visible transition seen by an incredible 16.9 million people.

Going forward after this surge of media exposure, my hope is that Caitlyn can go on with her life being happy and true to herself. In addition, as such a visible persona, my hope is that she will do some good in helping the 700,000+ transgender people who suffer serious issues such as marginalization, lack of access to physical or mental health care, job discrimination, health problems, violence, and killings--among many other issues.

Despite the increasingly more balanced and enlightened media coverage, the transgender population is still very much misunderstood, misrepresented, and marginalized by the media.

Although transgender is at the moment the topic du jour, it's now important that the other transgender voices are heard — those who are regularly discriminated against. That should be and likely will be the next area of media and societal focus as we get beyond one famous woman.

This discussion is not just about being transgender; it's about evolution and about us as a world understanding what this all means. Clearly, more needs to be done.

9. Transgender Children

The notion of transgender children is a complex topic on its own and beyond the scope of this book. However, it is a growing area of focus by society and the media. Many ask if children have a sense of their gender identity. Scientists now believe that gender identity is solidified around age four or five. If it doesn't match up with the sex they are assigned at birth, then that starts to manifest itself in different ways. This is being covered more frequently by the media, and increasingly, in a more balanced and researched way.

Of particular note is a book called *My Princess Boy* by Cheryl Kilodavis and illustrated by Suzanne DeSimone about tolerance and acceptance among children. The book shares the story of Cheryl's son Dyson, a 4-year-old boy who happily expresses his authentic self by dressing up in dresses and enjoying traditional girl things, such as jewelry and anything pink or sparkly.

Inspired by the author's son and her own initial struggles to understand, this is a heartwarming story about unconditional love and one remarkable family. It's also a call for an end to bullying and judgments. The book concludes with the understanding that "my" Princess Boy is really "our" Princess Boy, and as a community, we can accept and support youth for whoever they are and however they wish to look. Although there are way too many programs about transgender children to include here, some recent examples from around the world include:

On TV:

- *Transgender Girl Coy Mathis, 6, Tells Her Story to Katie Couric,* http://www.ontopmag.com/article.aspx?id=14507&MediaType=1&Category=16

- *Huffington Post: Sadie, 11-Year-Old Transgender Girl, Writes Essay In Response to Obama's Inauguration Speech* http://www.huffingtonpost.com/2013/01/23/transgender-girl-obama-speech_n_2533298.html#slide=2016213

- CBS-TV: *How more and more children are seeking treatment for GID at an earlier age* — http://www.cbsnews.com/8301-204_162-57381241/sex-change-treatment-for-kids-on-the-rise/

- *Washington Post Review* — http://voices.washingtonpost.com/blog-post/2010/10/princess_boy.html

- *Manchester Evening News: I want to help transgender people like me, says teenager 'trapped in wrong body* — http://www.manchestereveningnews.co.uk/news/greater-manchester-news/want-help-transgender-people-like-1738959

In books:

- *Gender Born, Gender Made: Raising Healthy Gender-Nonconforming Children* by Diane Ehrensaft PhD (May 17, 2011) A groundbreaking guide to caring for children who live outside binary gender boxes

- *My Princess Boy* by Cheryl Kilodavis and Suzanne DeSimone (Dec 21, 2010)

- *The Transgender Child: A Handbook for Families and Professionals* by Stephanie Brill and Rachel Pepper (2008)

SECTION FOUR

Understanding and Acceptance

1. Judgment & Belittlement

"Love isn't a state of perfect caring. It is an active noun like 'struggle.' To love someone is to strive to accept that person exactly the way he or she is, right here and now."
—Fred Rogers

Wow! Mr. Rogers got it. I wish we could just live in his neighborhood and all get along. So many people make judgments based on what they don't know. They tend to have animosity toward whatever they're ignorant about. Transgender isn't the problem. The problem is society's responses to it.

Most people don't know that I am transgender, likely because they've had little exposure to, or context of transgender people, or if they suspect I am transgender, they don't say anything, possibly out of respect or politeness, or as I suspect, they simply don't know. If I do present myself as trans, the reaction is consistent, ranging from, "I didn't know," to "I kind of thought you were, but I wasn't sure." Either way, I rarely feel any lack of acceptance from most people. And if I did, I am way past being concerned about it.

Interestingly, for the paucity of friends or family members who have not accepted me, I suspect that in some cases, it's more about their own insecurities regarding gender, sexual orientation, body type, religious customs, and/or general lack of knowledge and understanding about gender identity. But I really don't know.

However, if I were to be belittled in any way, I simply would say, "I'm sorry you feel that way." To me, my "sorrow" expresses a sense of genuine empathy towards the other person, the "you" expresses transference and conveys that it's your problem, not mine; and the "feel that way" conveys being non-judgmental about how the other person feels, neither right or wrong. I've actually never had to say this, but it's what I would say if I were confronted.

Today, I'm happy (and very lucky) that I receive very positive responses from most of my family and so many friends from earlier in my life when I inform them of my "minor" change. I'm not a Fred Rogers fanatic, and I understood that his acceptance of LGBTQ people evolved over time, but I admire what Teresa Heinz Kerry said about him at his funeral: "He never condescended, just invited us into his conversation. He spoke to us as the people we were, not as the people others wished we were." It is a *Beautiful Day in the Neighborhood.*

> *"I would like them to understand that we're people. We're*
> *human beings, and this is a human life."*
> —Andreja Pejic, model

2. Telling My Family

Telling my family I was transgender was difficult and came as a shock to them since I had always tried to fit in as a young "man" by presenting as male, wearing macho clothes, and projecting a guy-like persona to my friends, family, and colleagues. To them, I appeared to be happy.

Therefore, after opening up to my family, they essentially mourned the loss of a son and a brother. Eventually, as they got to know the "new" me, they realized that there was much more to life than "losing" the pants and ties and exchanging them for dresses and skirts that represented my inner self. They were gaining a family member who was finally aligned and authentic with herself. It went like this:

Sister Sally. During a long hike in the woods many years ago, the first sister who suspected something was different about me asked, "Are you wearing a bra?"

I said, "Yes."

She asked why.

I answered, "So that I don't bounce."

Although I think it was a perfectly reasonable, honest, and direct answer, it was the beginning of many discussions and gradual acceptance with her and eventually the rest of my family.

In telling brother Tom, I couched the news as part of two issues, the second being a faulty drainpipe at our shared family summer cabin. I told him my challenging news first. His response was, "What else?" I think he was more concerned about the pipe. Acceptance by him and his family continues through today.

Sister Sue. Another sister, after spending a weekend with me at our summer cabin years ago said, "Now that I've gotten to re-know you, I can't see you as anyone else but Carla."

Sister Liz. Much younger than me, said, after letting me know she had just told her young kids about me, said that both were totally unconcerned. In fact, her 13-year-old daughter had a transgender friend at her summer camp. And her 8-year-old son, whom I have always been very fond of, after we spent our traditional morning "hunting" for Indian arrowheads as myself, apparently told Liz he didn't see any difference. I guess as long as you can still hunt for arrowheads, (actually, I think we were filling bags with rocks), gender identity really doesn't matter. If only society could be so accepting.

Sister Barb. And one more sister, just a year younger than me, said in seeing me for the first time as myself said, after giving me a big hug, exclaimed, "You don't look any different!" I guess all the years of dressing nicely and applying nice makeup didn't kick in. Oh, well.

I also have a very large extended family on my father's side, due to his younger brother, Donald and older sister, Lois (Geertz). Today I have my wonderful Aunt Mary, seven cousins (from Don and Mary); two remaining cousins from Lois—Kathy and John—and a whole next generation or two of an extended family of millions of more kids.

Front row: Laura, Gretchen, Paul. Second row: John Geertz, Karen, Jim. Back row: Bob, Nancy (Circa—a while back)

It took a long time for me to muster the courage to reach out to my extended family to let them know about my "minor" change, since those you love and care for the most are the toughest to tell, particularly family. As my cousin Karen later told me, "The mountain just gets farther away." However, this is very difficult because you have the most to lose if there is rejection. When I finally did tell them, shortly after the passing of my Uncle Don, whom I cared for deeply, it turned out that all my cousins had already known anyway, due to the fact that for years, I had spoken regularly with my aunt and uncle on the phone. What I didn't realize was that my name "Carla Anne" always appeared on their phone, so of course, they easily put it all together (along with a little help from Google and my tech-savvy cousins). I learned later from my cousins that my aunt and uncle had always felt that if and when I was ready to tell them about my gender identity, I would do so.

I finally did reach out to my cousins and was very lucky to find them understanding and accepting. I just wish my immediate family had been as accepting as my extended family. However, I also know it can be very difficult to understand and accept this when it is a sibling.

One of my cousins, Laura Ernst, who is much younger than me, lives in Wisconsin as well. We both have gone through significant life challenges and regularly give each other support. One time, Laura asked me for help moving to a new apartment, but was concerned that I didn't have the physical strength to do so. So I told her, "I still have the muscles of a man, but the emotions of a woman." I argued, she really gets two cousins in one. (Fortunately, she found some strapping young guys instead.)

I am also particularly close to my cousin Kathy (Geertz), who is my age and one of the most wonderful people ever made. Very kind, smart, and talented. She also is an RN. And although she was also an oboe player (a double-reed woodwind), and I am a clarinet player (a single-reed instrument), I've always worked to be good friends with double-reed players. (They just have stronger lips and better ears than we single-reed players.)

As children, Kathy and I spent our Christmas and Thanksgiving holiday dinners together, along with all of our cousins, at our grandparents Louie and Laura's home. Although Kathy and I seemed to have been perennially banished to the "little kids" table for those joyous events, we bonded for life there, mostly due to staring contests which I always lost to her. Today, when we convene for meals as adults, we instinctively pull out a card table and eat in the corner.

I care deeply for my extended family and am very thankful and happy to receive their bountiful understanding, acceptance, and love. My only regret was not having told them much earlier and more directly. As a communicator, I know the worst way to manage an issue is letting things leak out in drips and drabs, and not have it come directly from the source.

This is crisis communications 101. As my friend Richard C. Hyde, one of the country's top crisis communications professionals, once told me when I asked him how he always remained so calm in the heat of battle when plants were blowing up and planes falling from the sky, "What is the secret to effective crisis communications?"

He calmly said, "Well, you get all the information out, quickly and accurately." Sounds simple enough. I guess I should have had him handle my internal family communications.

Things are a bit better now. However, I think the essence of this kicks in when we all convene each summer for vacation at our third-generation Wisconsin family summer cottage. It comes down more to the expeditiousness, practicality, and needs of functioning effectively as a large family with day-to-day living in a small cabin. There, the main concerns are really much more about who's cooking the brats, whether or not there's enough butter for the fresh-picked corn, and perhaps most importantly (at least in Wisconsin), is if there's enough beer in the downstairs fridge. Having a transgender family member is one thing, but getting the brats soaked in beer, on the grill, and cooked is another. (Welcome to Wisconsin.)

Bratwurst on the grill—a visual for readers
outside Wisconsin.

3. What I Wear (on the Outside)

*"Consider that people will talk about the fact that
I now 'pass' as a woman, but nobody ever asks
about how difficult it must have been for me to
'pass' as a man before."*
—Julia Serano, author, performer

The gender expressions I present through clothing, makeup, jewelry, and mannerisms are my own for the choosing. While I may be treated "differently" by society for presenting as more feminine, masculine, or more androgynously, I have to take into account my own comfort levels, sense of style, and sensibilities.

But as my friends from childhood realized I was happier, more social, more productive, getting better clients, performing more music, and just living my life as the woman I am, I stopped seeing signs of grief. They perceive my inner sense of happiness, which, to me, is much more vital than what I wear or how I present.

I've long since come to realize that the gender assigned to me at birth as a male was a "promise" to others as to who I was, but was not something I could keep trying to be.

The hurt you experience by those you think are the closest to you and you care about the most—as they are hating you—cause you to live in hiding, making you feel you're surrounded by shame and humiliation. My body simply did not match my brain and inner self. I had the external body of a male (at least at one point in my life), but I've always had the brain, feelings, identity, and sensibilities of a female.

You can't help to wonder why this happened, why your mind is completely different than what you were born as, but it is unquestionably what it is. For those who are not familiar with the needs and feelings of transgender persons, it's like any other group looking for acceptance from not only society, but from themselves as they continue on their own path of discovery. It's difficult for non-transgender people to grasp this.

I eventually spent time reaching out to all my friends and contacts from throughout my life—from childhood through college—to let them know about my "minor change." Typical responses were:

- "I can only imagine the courage required to make this change, but it sounds like you're now in a good place." – Bob S

- "I'm happy that your realization came to pass at a time in your life that will allow you to be YOU." – Fred H

- "I'm so glad you've become what makes you feel complete and happy...you are a very lucky woman!" – Sue T

- "There's nothing better than knowing and seeing a friend pursue and become their true self." – Hiroshi W

- You look great and sound very happy – I'm psyched about it! – Wald H

- "Love you and that you are living your truth! I would hope that your more than "minor change" would have and most likely has made you a superior human being! – Susan B

- "I'm happy that you've been able to finally be your true self!" – Toby S

- The world is already a better place because of people like you. Good for you, Carla! – Jane F

And finally,

- "It's a girl thing…we rock the world!!" – Wendy S.

> *"It is an awful thing to be betrayed by your body. And it's lonely because you feel you can't talk about it. You feel it's something between you and the body. You feel it's a battle you will never win . . . and yet you fight it day after day and it wears you down. Even if you try to ignore it, the energy it takes to ignore it will exhaust you."*
> —David Levithan, author

4. Trans Friends

I have dozens of trans friends across America and have had them for a long time. Transgender people are so commonplace to me, I have to be reminded that there are many who are not familiar with trans people, causing me to be on "guard" for potential minimization, prejudice, and harassment.

Sadly, if you look at the daily headlines centered on transgender, you'll find horrific stories about harassment, torture, bullying, suicide, and brutal killings. It's difficult to understand this disconnect when I know so many wonderful transgender people as decent, caring, smart, successful, loving, and productive human beings from all walks of life. I never see them as trans people, but rather just as people with the same kinds of interests and concerns anyone else has.

The prevalence of suicide attempts among respondents to the National Transgender Discrimination Survey (NTDS), conducted by the National Gay and Lesbian Task Force and National Center for Transgender Equality, is 41 percent, which vastly exceeds the 4.6 percent of the overall U.S. population who report a lifetime suicide attempt, and is also higher than the 10 to 20 percent of lesbian, gay and bisexual adults who report ever attempting suicide.

I lost two close friends to suicide within the last year. Both were trans women. Both took their own lives. The second one hit me particularly hard. Her name was Karis. She is the person to whom I dedicated this book.

It happened last Thanksgiving. I think what I posted on Facebook when I first realized what had happened sums up my feelings then and still feel relevant for me today:

Karis Anne Ross

I started seeing FB missives last night as the horror of the messages struck like daggers throughout my body—only hoping it couldn't be true. Now my uncontrollable tears burst out as the reality set in. I could not have been more stunned. I can't come close to putting into words how sad I feel. This will probably take a very long time to absorb and accept if ever. A beautiful life snuffed out when her flame was just starting to sparkle.

A talented teacher, woman of the world, funny, warm-hearted and genuine soul who always made us smile. I loved Karis deeply, but Karis was someone who loved us all and we all loved her. Her absence will be a silent grief for a long time.

It's the many times we spent together, helping each other follow our dreams. Karis gave the most precious gifts in life— listening and understanding, caring and love—gifts that only come from the heart. For us that knew her, it will be about the love we share in her memory, the comfort we lend to each other and the need to help each other at this difficult time. Our hearts are broken. She will be greatly missed. Rest in peace, darling. We loved you, Karis.

Karis Anne Ross

As an addendum to my lost friend Karis, there was a life celebration about seven months after her death. This was what I conveyed on Facebook then, shortly after attending this very sad event:

Yesterday I attended a Life Celebration for my friend Karis Ross, who was taken away from us last November. Words are difficult to find for the emotionally powerful celebration of an incredible woman, an incredible human being who left us way too soon. Among a crowd of at least 100 people, I heard so much about her from so many people, showing how much she was loved by so many, and learning only then what a multi-faceted and talented person she was on so many levels.

The outpouring of love, kindness and remembrance was overwhelming, staged in a beautiful park setting on the bluffs of Lake Michigan just South of Milwaukee. I'll never forget this tribute to an amazing woman, and I will never forget Karis. As one person said, "We all carry a little bit of Karis with us as she touched so many of us."

We will miss her.

> *"Rejecting your gay or transgender child won't make them straight. It will only mean you will lose them."*
> —Christina Engela, author

5. Our Trans Family

On a more positive note, I was recently asked to participate as a subject in a photo exhibition called *Our Trans Family*, featuring photographs of some 30 transgender people and their families (www.facebook.com/events/1780017122270472).

The purpose of the exhibition was to foster greater understanding about people who identify as transgender in Wisconsin. The project also included a broad range of people who identify as "gender fluid," as well as those who do not identify with a binary definition of their gender.

It was photographed by three experienced documentary photographers, Meredith Watts (photographer of the picture on the cover of this book), Jeff Pearcy, and Rikki Thompson. Although it's not an effort to stress assimilation, the emphasis was to create images and text that captured the worth and dignity of transgender people in

"Carla is a jazz musician in Milwaukee and appears in the photo exhibition, *Our Trans Family*, opening Friday, November 4, 2016 at the Kenilworth Square East Gallery courtesy of the University of Wisconsin-Milwaukee's Peck School of the Arts."

an effort to provide a better understanding of the basic humanity of transgender people.

In addition, it was designed to portray people in the transgender community as they express themselves, along with the support of their natural or chosen families of support.

Although I was honored to be asked to be included in the exhibition, it actually was a surprisingly difficult decision to make to agree to participate, since I am relatively reticent about identifying as a transgender person. But hey, if you write a book about your life called *Life Without Pockets, My Long Journey into Womanhood*, that just may "out" me, too.

When the show was promoted using my image (with my permission), it automatically linked to my Facebook site, which does not present me as a transgender woman. So, when this occurred and my FB friends saw this, the reaction was interesting. About a third thought I still lived in New York, another third did not know I was a musician, and another third did not know I was a transgender woman. Well, they all know now!

At first, I was concerned about being "outed" and losing friends, but after reflecting on this, I decided that if someone were to "unfriend" me because I'm trans, then that person would not be my friend anyway.

I guess I'm now "out!"

6. What Do Trans People Talk About?

People have asked me what transgender people talk about. Well, like anyone else, they talk about a wide range of topics that interest them. This could be art, music, culture, great restaurants, sports, or politics, usually beyond the limited and somewhat worn-out topic (at least for me) of transgender.

At the same time, when I go out Thursday nights to what we affectionately call GNO (Girls' Night Out), it's remarkably liberating to be among trans or at least trans-friendly people who understand this, and being in a place you don't have to talk about it, or answer the same old tiresome questions over and over again. I guess it's a "let your hair down" kind of moment with the girls (since we all generally have long hair). And no one

Me and Girls' Night Out (GNO) friends.

in a group like this would ask, "Carla, what's it like to be transgender?"

Besides, it's fun to talk about girly things like clothes, makeup, cosmetics, and jewelry like any other woman might. And of course, weight loss—always a big topic among the girls. In fact, I'm trying to lose 30 pounds over the next three days. I even joined a gym, but unfortunately after 30 days, I had not lost one pound. All I lost were my glasses, so I called and complained. They said, "Carla, you actually have to come in." I was shocked. I had filled out all the forms and received all the incessant motivational "You Go Girl!" emails. They said to come in sometime so they could see less of me.

I should add, since hopefully no little children are reading this, is that I've been amused to sometimes hear trans women at various states of their transitions belly up to the bar and brag about how small their male parts are. Who would have thought!?

For me, my "GNO" nights are just a part of my life, in that most of my activities are with non-trans people and activities centered around many common interests such as music, literature, business, hiking, sailing, tennis, canoeing, movies, spirituality, history, ecology, social justice and work, volunteer activities, and many other goings on.

Also, like many transgender people, I can usually recognize other trans people where non-trans people often don't. However, this does not guarantee an automatic bonding and friendship, as you tend to become close to people you connect with and have something substantive in common. In fact, I find often that many trans people prefer to not hang out with other trans people in that they've moved beyond that, so I respect those feelings as well. Also, when multiple trans women are together, you most assuredly "look" trans. So, if that bothers a trans person, then best to not cluster!

7. God

Throughout my entire life, I've made a conscious effort to make my mental, emotional, physical, spiritual, and social wellbeing (MEPSS) be my guiding life principles. I believe that if the teachings of all the prophets could be boiled down into one word, it would be love.

I also try to eat healthy foods, I have a regular yoga and meditation practice, I've chosen career opportunities and volunteer work that are aligned with my soul's purpose, and I do my best to balance my work, personal, emotional, and spiritual life so that I can contribute to society and feel happy and fulfilled.

Going back to my earliest and darkest memories, I endured the belief that my faith was at odds with my gender identity, and I hid emotionally deep in the back pews of our large Catholic church. Through my spiritual journey, however, I discovered what God—or whatever spiritual force exists—is telling me: that who I am is a gift centered in my soul. I've now come to know that I need to trust in a higher being enough to be able to embrace my authentic self.

I believe that the essential moral and philosophical teachings associated with many religions are sound, but the dogmas and canons that often come with them often are not. Thus, I respect the teachings of many religions. Today, I'm an ardent follower of writers and prophets like Jesus of Nazareth, the Talmudic prophets, Baha'u'llah (founder of the Baha'i Faith), and the Buddha, among others. This means I try to live a moral and just life according their teachings. To me, if these figures could be summed up in one word, once again, I think it would come to the word love. And maybe some compassion as well.

Key principles of the church I go to are expressed in the words "Love is the Spirit of this Church . . . and to dwell together in peace, to seek the truth in love, and to help one another." Jesus said to love my neighbor, my enemy and do not judge. I also find that idea clearly articulated in the well-known writings of I Corinthians 13: 4-5: "Love is patient. Love is kind. It does not envy. It does not boast. It is not proud. It is not rude. It is not self-seeking. It is not easily angered. It keeps no record of wrongs." I believe that this passage first describes how God loves me.

In the "Bible Belt," there are tons of common misconceptions as to whether or not members of the LGBTQ community are Christians. Some people in the Christian community misinterpret this because in the New International Version (NIV) Bible in 1Corinthians 6:9, there was a mistranslation of the Greek word *arsenokoitai* within the verse. It was likely mistranslated as the word "homosexual," when in reality, it was and is associated with the definition of being an affiliated or an affiliate of prostitution. And it certainly was never associated with the transgender community.

In the Christian Bible, binary gender (division into male and female) isn't clearly defined with words such as "man" or "woman" until the 22nd verse of the second chapter of Genesis. Before that division, Genesis 2 refers to the first human as *"ha'adam,"* a "creature made of earth."

According to the Gospel of Matthew in Chapter 19, Jesus refers to what is likely a transgender person as a "natural-born eunuch." Also, in Galatians 3:28, "There's neither Jew nor Greek, there is neither slave nor free, there is no male and female, for you are all one in Christ Jesus."

This is not a treatise to support one way or another whether or not Christian theology supports or rejects transgenderism, as it certainly is not stated one way or another. This is rather to point out that it is surely open for interpretation, as it has already been extensively written about by numerous bible scholars and others, and with contradictory conclusions.

Being transgender is not a sin or pathology. Based on science, it's uncommon, but normal and natural. For example, in 1Chronicles 29 it says, "For all things come of thee, oh Lord." I would ask if science is a gift from God, why should we not respect who we are and how we are made?

However, for me, in coming to that understanding, I ultimately removed the spiritual blockade to being able to receive

God's love as it was intended—unconditionally. Now I can get on about the business of learning how better to love others in the way it is intended—unconditionally.

God views people like me as He (or She) does anyone else, with love and delight. God upholds His grace and truth through love. The fact that some individuals are born with signs of genetic variation in their sex-determining genes and chromosomes does not change their value in God's eyes, any more than someone born with the mutation that causes cystic fibrosis or sickle-cell anemia, or another pre-designated category such as race or ethnicity.

I know quite a few other trans people, many of them spiritually and/or religiously based. I don't pass judgment on them or anyone else, as I know they often struggle as well. But if we look to the Christian Bible, it says in Romans, 14:10, "You, then, why do you judge your brother or sister? Or why do you treat them with contempt? For we will all stand before God's judgment seat … therefore let us stop passing judgment on one another. Instead, make up your mind not to put any stumbling block or obstacle in the way of a brother or sister."

Pope Francis has made significant strides in preaching for greater inclusion and acceptance of all human beings. Named *TIME* magazine's "Person of the Year" in 2013, the Pontiff said, "Who am I to judge a gay or transgender person of goodwill who seeks the Lord? You can't marginalize these people." Although you would not characterize the Pope as being pro-LGBTQ, by today's standards, his influence would be more significant within the Catholic church among those who often convey the most fervid opposition.

Bishop Christopher Coyne

Vermont Roman Catholic Bishop Christopher Coyne conveyed that not only would he welcome transgender people in church, he also acknowledges the evidence that trans people do not choose to be transgender. "There's increasing evidence that a lot of this is biological ... that transgender people are really struggling with the idea of gender identity ... and that's through no fault of their own. This is who they are. Everyone is one of God's creatures. I would invite anyone to come to the table."

Allyson Robinson

The Baptist church recently ordained West Point transgender graduate Allyson Robinson, a human rights advocate who held rank as captain in the U.S. Army. Before her gender reassignment, Robinson was married to Danyelle Robinson, with whom she has four children and is still happily married.

She said, "I would conclude that understanding, acceptance, respect, and love need to begin somewhere. Since it exists among our own community, it seems it should also be so in the Christian faith, where love is the key principle of Christian life—a sharing in the fullness of love, the personal divine-human communion that Christ represents."

Her unique story is told on an informative TedTalk at www.youtube.com/watch?v=SCpHCGniGiI.

Unitarian Universalists, Baha'i and other Faiths

Unitarian Universalists (UUs) are guided in their living faith
with their "Principles and Purposes," which point out how
Jewish and Christian teachings call us to "respond to God's love
by loving our neighbors as ourselves." UUs are also guided by,
"Words and deeds of prophetic women and men that challenge
us to confront powers and structures of evil with justice, compassion, and the transforming power of love."

Unitarian Universalists are unified by their shared search for
spiritual growth. They affirm that from these traditions comes a
deep regard for intellectual freedom and inclusive love, so that
congregations and members seek inspiration and derive insight
from all major world religions, emphasizing "the spiritual unity
of all humankind."

In the teachings of the Bahá'í faith, a monotheistic world
religion, founder Baha'u'llah emphasizes that "Love is the most
great law that rules this mighty and heavenly cycle. It is the
unique power that binds together the diverse elements of this
material world, it is the supreme magnetic force that directs the
movements of the spheres in the celestial realms." He proclaims
that, "Love is light in whatsoever house it may shine and enmity
is darkness in whatsoever abode it dwell."

In the Buddhist tradition, love is one of the primary paths to
full spiritual liberation. Buddhist love includes those forms of
love characterized by freedom. Buddhism is based on the
development of mindfulness through the practice of meditation
and cultivation of higher wisdom and discernment, particularly
through the precepts centered on non-violence, honesty, mind-

fulness and nutritional balance. The Buddha says, "In the end, only three things matter: how much you loved, how gently you lived, and how gracefully you let go of things not meant for you."

8. My Spiritual Beliefs

Benjamin Franklin

In terms of my own beliefs, I continually find that they align most closely with the views of Ben Franklin, who wrote on March 9, 1790 (a month before his death) in a letter to Ezra Stiles, then President of Yale College, his final and most famous description of his personal faith:

> "I believe in one God, creator of the Universe. That he governs it in his providence. That he ought to be worshipped. That the most acceptable service we can render to Him is doing good to his other Children. That the soul of Man is immortal, and will be treated with Justice in another Life respecting its conduct in this. These I take to be the fundamental Principles of all sound Religion, and I regard them as you do in whatever Sect I meet with them. As to Jesus of Nazareth, I think the System of Morals and his Religion, as he left them to us, the best the World ever saw or is likely to see; but I apprehend that it has received various corrupting changes, and I have, with most of the present Dissenters in England, some Doubts as to his Divinity; tho' it is a question I do not dogmatize upon, having never studied it, and think it needless to busy myself with it now, when expect soon an Opportunity of knowing the Truth with less Trouble. I shall only add,

respecting myself, that, having experienced the Goodness of that Being in conducting me prosperously thro' a long life, I have no doubt of its Continuance in the next, though without the smallest Conceit of meriting such Goodness."

I could not have said it better. And due to my continually advancing age and thinning hair, I'm beginning to see an increasingly closer physical resemblance to Mr. Franklin. Besides, I grew up in the age of electricity. In my day, when you turned off a light switch, it never said, "Are you sure you want to turn it off?" It never had memory issues, had to be re-booted, or said, "You've created a fatal error." Fatal? Seems a bit extreme. I guess it's a brave new world.

> *"Nature chooses who will be transgender; individuals don't choose this."*
> —Mercedes Ruehl

9. Man or Woman?

People have asked me, "What constitutes a 'real woman?'" I simply respond, "How am I not one?" Is it because of my chromosomes? My body? My mind? My female identity?

In terms of chromosomes, I don't think so, since my extra X indicates both male and female. Even if I didn't have an extra X chromosome, that means little to me.

From an anatomical perspective, I've known plenty of women who did not develop breasts at puberty. Did they say, "I don't have breasts, so I must be a man?" And my GG female friends who've suffered through and survived breast cancer and double mastectomies—do they think they are no longer women? I don't think so.

And what about men whose male anatomy did not develop as robustly as they might otherwise had hoped? Did they too comparably ask, "Am I a woman?" I don't think so. Gender identity is linked integrally to one's inner sense of maleness or femaleness, not so much to one's body.

Therefore, I ask, is the reason someone wants to disqualify me from womanhood related to the fact that I don't have a fully formed uterus and can't birth a child? And if so, do they also reject womanhood of infertile women or those who have had miscarriages or hysterectomies?

Jaclyn Schultz, Miss Michigan 2013, was born with "ambiguous genitalia," but not with a fully formed uterus. This is known as Mayer-Rokitansky-Küster-Hauser syndrome (MRKH). She was born perfectly healthy, with the exception of her missing uterus (also causing an inability to menstruate).

Does the fact that I wasn't socialized consistently as a woman mean I need to be excluded from womanhood today? Is it that I was partially (but maybe not effectively) socialized as a man for part of my life, force me to become a man?

I sincerely doubt that most people would so much as question the womanhood of the women I described. After all, it's not their choice or "fault" that they were born with anomalies. How am I any different? I didn't choose to be male, female, or transgender. I just am.

> *"We make assumptions every day about other people's genders without ever seeing their birth certificates, chromosomes, genitals, reproductive systems, childhood socialization, or their legal sex. There is no such thing as a "real" gender – there's only the gender we experience ourselves as and the gender we perceive others to be."*
> —Julia Serano, PhD, author, performer

10. Hormones

Not all transgender people take hormones. But for those who do, it's a two-part process. To help feminize a genetic male, it's important to suppress production of the male hormone testosterone. The other part is the administration of estrogen, the chief hormone at work in biological females.

Unlike their M2F counterparts, trans men don't have to take any estrogen-suppressing substances as part of their hormone treatments. Testosterone (typically just called "T" in the community) is a powerful hormone, and the raising of testosterone levels in a trans man overpowers existing estrogen levels.

For me, after many years of transition, a new job, a move to Milwaukee, being a medical patient of an awesome primary-care physician and therapist at a wonderful T-friendly family health clinic in a Hispanic neighborhood with a specialty in gender-related issues, I've had the opportunity to have hormone replacement therapy. Easy enough. I've also become active in the trans-community and PFLAG (the original ally organization made up of parents, families, friends and straight allies uniting with LGBTQ people), Pride Fest, and to some extent the local LGBTQ center.

I had taken for years the medication Spironolactone to reduce the testosterone in my system, plus weekly transdermal infusions of estradiol, a common form of estrogen found in pubescent and post-pubescent women. Being an anti-androgen, Spironolactone works to decrease the body's testosterone output, while estradiol increases estrogen levels. This is administered by an integrated team of transgender-savvy doctors and therapists at my terrific medical clinic. It's too bad that I didn't start this when I was much younger, as so many young people do today, and I wish I had had the knowledge and resources people have now. But it is what it is and I'm happy to be where I am and who I am today.

> "Accepted social gender roles and expectations are so entrenched in our culture that most people cannot imagine any other way. As a result, individuals fitting neatly into these expectations rarely if ever question what gender really means. They have never had to, because the system has worked for them."
> —Nicki Petrikowski, author

11. Harmony, Joy, and Contentment

When I first underwent hormone therapy, I'd begun to experience the physical and mental impact of the hormones, genetics, and chromosomes a couple of years into it—and with it, a new sense of clarity, inner peace, and happiness for the first time in my life. My mind and body began to interconnect as one for the first time.

Over time, this has created some pleasant physical and psychological developments. With every passing day (so to speak), looking into the mirror, I'd see someone who looked more like my internal sense of self and less like the stranger I had seen earlier in my life. I finally began to feel "right" on an emotional level. The jarring dissonance between my brain and the chemicals around it finally began to fade, leaving me in a place of harmony, joy, and happiness. I can only describe it as the peaceful feeling you get when you first hear a beautiful piece of music or read a moving poem.

In a recent *Vanity Fair* interview, contributing editor Patricia Bosworth, who interviewed models from a recent Barney's ad campaign featuring transgender people, model Arin Andrews explained how his transition changed him: "You have this new love for life. You want to make something of yourself because you struggled hard to survive. The experiences I went through made me into the guy I am today. I think that's the best thing about this: I am the man I want to be." I can relate.

"The whole point of my gender transition was to free myself up. If something feels right, I'm not going to stop doing it because it doesn't fit someone else's notion of what a man or woman is."
—David Harrison, playwright, actor

12. Friendship

"Friends can help each other. A true friend is someone who lets you have total freedom to be yourself - and especially, to feel. Or, not feel. Whatever you happen to be feeling at the moment is fine with them. That's what real love amounts to--letting a person be what he or she really is."
—Jim Morrison, The Doors

Friends have always been important me, and this condition certainly tests the strength and value of a friendship. The good news: the people I call my friends with deep, long-lasting relationships have not only accepted me, but seem to detect my authenticity and feel that is far more important than trying to hide the real me from them.

Over the past thirty years or so, I methodically but reticently conveyed to all my friends and family, particularly those from my more distant past, who I was inside. I took a somewhat deliberate and segmented approach reaching out to specific groups. For the most part, this went far better than I thought it would. Although I feared judgment, criticism, and outright hatred, surprisingly, I found considerable understanding and acceptance, and in a few cases—was surprised by "confessions" from friends who also were in various states of LGBTQ transition.

One group included current friends and acquaintances generally from my life today. They, of course, only knew me as a woman. If I occasionally felt compelled to tell someone I had once lived as a man, they simply did not believe it, saying they could not imagine me as a male.

In contrast, I reached out and told longtime friends from my earliest days—childhood, high school, college, and work colleagues—that I had gone through a "minor change" since I last saw them, and I now am a woman. Same problem, but the reverse. They could not imagine me as a woman. I think that this is more due to it being an abstract concept in their minds and not being able to know me today as myself. However, I've found that when they meet me today and see me as myself, they feel more comfortable and accepting.

Today, younger people are much more exposed to the notion of transgender and gender fluidity. They typically accept it with considerable ease, often knowing many LGBTQ people, or are gender fluid themselves. Older people seem to vary from being somewhat knowledgeable to having virtually no exposure but are often interested in knowing more about it.

People often attribute words such as "brave" and "courageous" to me. I wish I could say I have those virtues but being more of a complete and utter chicken and outright scaredy-cat, "brave" and "courageous" are wonderful attributes, but I am neither.

People often ask me how I chose my name. In reality, I didn't —it seemed to choose me. As long as I can remember, I have known Carla was my name. Perhaps like a lot of transgender women, they end up with names similar or feminized versions of their former male name. Although there is connective tissue between my former name and I like to say "my real name," I really don't know how I knew that was my name—but I inherently just knew. Regardless, Carla Ernst is my name now— mentally, emotionally, socially, and legally.

Some friends have expressed jealousy that I am living my authentic life, as they too have had long-held secrets regarding their sense of gender or sexuality they've always wanted to share or realize. Oddly, they tend to share them with me due to a high comfort and/or trust level, and/or feeling that they have tacit "permission" to discuss intimate feelings with me since I'm transgender. Yet they stay in the closet for fear of lack of acceptance from society and continue to deal instead with some degree of angst. For the most part, though, I've been extremely surprised at the overall acceptance of my being the person I am.

When I told one of my former work colleagues about my "minor gender change," he said, "As long as what's between your ears is the same, I'm OK with it." I told him it's the same, just that my ears are much cuter now. And they're pierced.

When I told my two daughters that I was a woman, they each responded, "I know." They not only accepted me, they also seemed to have always innately known I was a woman, adding that I had a "feminine persona." In fact, today they call me their GVP (Gender-Variant Parent).

Our only challenge is how to handle Mother's or Father's Day since I'm not either, so one daughter is advocating a "GVP Day." I'm sure Hallmark would embrace that idea. wish society was as open, understanding, accepting, and loving as my own daughters.

13. Betrayal

I think one of the biggest fears for a transgender person is to look into the eyes of close, long-time friends and family and tell them who you really are. Who you've always been. Whether they knew it or not. This can be completely paralyzing.

For me, it was difficult to leave the security of hiding who I was to potentially be judged by lifelong friends. The perennial issue is around what you need to share about your gender dysphoria to whom, how much, when, why, and how. This becomes very complex. But I would ask—like any other personal condition—who would ever be compelled to meet someone new and say, "Hi, my name is Carla and I'm a transgender woman." Who cares? (Guess what, they generally don't!)

For friends and family, the people you've known the longest and care about the most, the problem I've found is more about betrayal, since those people typically feel they have the "right" to know first. The dilemma is that these are the people you have the most to lose from on a personal, emotional, and possibly professional level, let alone the mental stress of a painful rejection from someone you care about. Thus, the mountain tends to get farther and farther away as you procrastinate in telling them.

I've experienced this firsthand and lost one of my oldest and best friends, who felt betrayed by me for not telling him a long time ago or first. I attempted to express the difficulty and fear of discussing this, but it not only landed on deaf ears, but after a very long conversation, it prompted an accusatory reaction, telling me I was a "f___ ing coward" to not have told him. So that went well.

Actually, that was probably the most hurtful and painful part of this entire gender journey, and has taken me a very long time to process and recover from.

Being transgender is not something you can easily hide, thus it can and will get out, thus robbing you of the opportunity to tell those you care for. Either telling them directly, preventing the third-party rumor mill to tell the story for you, which can be, and invariably will be, far worse. For those you care less about (and if for some reason, you even choose to tell them,) you have little to lose, thus it's easy to tell them.

> *"Outside of a dog, a book is a man's best friend.*
> *Inside of a dog, well it's too dark to read."*
> —Groucho Marx

14. A Woman's Best Friend

My life partner and guard dog Louie is a "Beagle Mix." An American foxhound with a beagle face, according to his (somewhat dubious) purebred "papers" from the rescue shelter. (I'm now convinced it was a typo—I think they meant "pure bread.") I don't know if a mutt can have "papers." However, he was initially scooped up in North Carolina, so at least is ADS (American Deep Southern). This is indicated when he howls at fire engines and goes "*HowloohYouAll.*"

Clearly a Southern dog, Louie is lovable but not brilliant. He's a few peas short of a casserole. He's got the attention span of a lightning bolt. When I look deep into his eyes, I see the back of his head. And out his ears. During the day, he chases parked cars, then sits on my TV and watches the sofa. He spends most of his time on dogbook.com. It's not healthy. I told him to get out more. But being a foxhound, he does keep me fox-free. Not a single fox in my house. He's my life partner that never grows up.

Louie is extremely mellow. If he could speak, his one word would be "whatever." He doesn't think back beyond three seconds, nor worry about the future. He lives totally in the moment. I think he's a Buddhist.

Louie sleeps with me at night for about 10 minutes until he thinks I'm asleep, and then quietly tiptoes—backwards—into his dog bed. I had a talk with him last night and gently explained,

"Louie, Milwaukee is a small town. People will talk. We can't be found sleeping together. So we'll have to be 'just friends.'"

Louie Ernst, my guard dog at work

He took it like a dog and has adjusted well to our new relationship. I've also had to have the little "talk" with him to let him know he was adopted. Although people have always said I have his nose, I assured him that although not biological, I was his loving and caring parent. He just said, "Whatever."

I've been taking him to Central Bark Dog School. Times being what they are, I had to pull him out. I'm now home-schooling him. He's doing well. He's got about a seven-word vocabulary: the usual dog words—*sit, stay, walk, heel.* I'm now wondering, since hound dogs max out at around seven words, why didn't I teach him words like, "Make the bed" . . . "Cook dinner ..." "Get a job" "Pay the mortgage"? But Louie readily accepts me for who I am. He doesn't care if I'm a man or a woman. Male or female. A few dog bones and a regular walk—he's good.

I learned a lot more about transgender people. It's not a choice, but a physiological condition that has to do with the size of the hypothalamus part of the brain.
—Mercedes Ruehl

15. Why?

Why am I like this? Frankly, I don't know.

Apart from the countless references throughout recorded history about hermaphrodites, two-spirited persons, third gender, intersex, androgyny, and biblically-expressed eunuchs, there are only theories about the causes of transgenderism conveyed in modern medicine.

One of the most prominent theories is a 2006 study published in the journal *Psychoneuroendocrinology* by Harald J. Schneider, Johanna Pickel, and Günter K. Stalla. That research suggests that there is a direct link between the amount of testosterone exposed to a fetus in utero and transgenderism.

Prenatal exposure to androgens (hormones that regulate the development and maintenance of male characteristics in both men and women) has been implicated in transgenderism, but the etiology of the condition remains unclear.

In other words, before my birth, I may have been exposed to too little testosterone while in my mother's womb, causing my brain to develop differently than that of the average baby male. But I don't know that. Another theory suggests that an imbalance occurs that results in a male embryo having a feminized brain during the period in utero when hormones help shape gender.

Other studies conducted by a consortium of institutions including Vanderbilt University Medical Center, George Washington University, and Boston Children's Hospital, are looking to the genome which has provided hints of a biological origin to causing transgenderism. Interestingly, although genetic considerations may be at play while digging into my extended family in researching this book, I learned of a male second cousin my same age with a shared great-grandfather who has the same transgender identity as I.

Regardless, I don't know what causes me being transgender. I know that if I did have a choice, I would not like to be transgender.

16. Choice?

Let's get back to the one word that initiated this book: *choice*. No matter the cause, transgender is, and has always been, a part of me. It's not a choice I made nor a "lifestyle" I chose, nor would I have if I could. If I could have, I would have chosen to be born congruent in mind and body. I didn't choose this, but I'm making the best of what I have and who I am.

There's no universal "trans narrative." My experience is mine alone. Every trans person has a unique life history. The more these stories are shared, the better society will be. There are situations that still frustrate me.

"Do we have to know who's gay and who's straight?
Can't we just love everybody and judge them
by the car they drive?"
—Ellen DeGeneres

Life Without Pockets

17. Am I Transgender Anymore?

Having become a woman, I now ask, "Am I even transgender anymore?" I have many trans friends at all stages of their transition. I always work to be helpful to anyone who seeks it, but I've essentially related to simply being a woman. I lost the capacity to see myself as a male anymore. It's rarely top of mind, regardless of all the changes I've gone through. It's odd now to sometimes feel marginalized out of the very marginalized group of which I am supposed to be a member. All I know for sure is there's been a change in me that can never be undone. I cannot stand up as anyone other than who I am.

18. Focus & Blossoming

As the cloud around my existence has for the most part long since lifted and slowly drifted away, I find myself able to focus in ways that I'd never been able to before. I became more caring and emotionally available. My work and level of happiness improved as a result of no longer feeling like my personal world and sense of identity were collapsing.

As I evolved into becoming my true self, I immersed myself in the passions and endeavors from earlier parts of my life — music performance, music composition, writing, career, sailing,

188 | Carla Anne Ernst

reading, tennis, social justice volunteer work, connecting deeply with friends and family, and spiritual pursuits.

Probably every passion and activity that's been important to me has come back into my life, except perhaps gymnastics (I was on my high school team). But I've accepted the fact that I won't likely qualify for the U.S. Olympic Team. At least not this year.

> *Accepted social gender roles and expectations are so entrenched in our culture that most people cannot imagine any other way. As a result, individuals fitting neatly into these expectations rarely if ever question what gender really means. They have never had to, because the system has worked for them."*
> —Nicki Petrikowski, author

19. Funerals

A unique event occurred that tested my transition and acceptance by life-long friends. A 93-year-old family friend named Bob G passed away in the community in which I grew up. He was the father of three grown children. The children have always been good friends, one of whom is named Steve, who has been one of my best friends since as early as I can remember.

Their father was also like a second father to me, as was his wife Nancy, who was like a second mother (she had passed several years earlier). Our families were also good friends with each other—interwoven into the fabric of our small community among schools, clubs, sports, vacations, churches, and social activities indigenous to suburban community life.

The family had exposed me early on to pursuits outside those of my own family, most notably sailing. They initiated my life-long passion for the sport. Further, the relationship ignited my journey into other areas such as electronics and amateur radio. An ongoing interest in Jungian philosophy. An early under-standing of the import of social justice. Attempts of tapping into the occult (failed attempts). Classical music, go-carts, motorcy-cles, and merriment generally associated with the travails of growing up. I loved (and still do) the entire family, as they instilled many of the values, interests, and passions rooted in me today.

After more decades than I care to admit, I was lucky enough to reconnect with the youngest "kid" brother, John, some six years my junior and now a grown man, psychologist, neighbor, great friend, and fellow church member—along with his won-derful wife Diana and their adult kids.

Despite the close relationship between our families, I was hesitant to attend his father's funeral back in my hometown. It would be difficult for me to have to confront the broader group of multi-generational family friends, and I didn't want the funeral to be about me.

I had three terrible options—none great. I considered "flip-flopping," i.e., trying to attend dressed as the male that many people once knew me as, or not attend at all. However, John encouraged me to attend—as myself—which I did.

Overall, the experience was as heartwarming as a funeral can be, and a generally positive experience for me to connect with so many childhood friends who were very supportive of me.

One exception, however, was an incident with one of the "moms" of the community. Since my mother was not able to attend the funeral due to health reasons, the senior mom decided to write my mother in Florida and tell her how much she enjoyed meeting her daughter, "Carla." The only problem was that my close-to-90-year-old mother did not know she had a daughter named Carla, nor would likely remember the circumstances of my intersex birth.

I had learned of this potential letter from a childhood friend of mine and son of the mom. He asked me if my mother knew about "transition." I told him no. I had previously decided not to convey this to her, feeling that someone in their golden years did not need to know about the complexities of gender dysphoria. I asked that he share my feelings with his mother, that I hoped she would use her discretion about a highly sensitive issue, and that I preferred that she not send the letter. Well, discretions with-standing, she sent the letter anyway. Two of my sisters were with my mother when she received the letter. My mother read it and burst into tears, feeling she had lost a son. (That went well.)

In damage-control mode, I called her immediately and was forced to tell her about me. However, after some initial shock and a long conversation, the conversation went better than I had anticipated. My mother's concerns evolved to two issues: one, was I making money. And two, and most surprisingly, her maternal instincts kicked in and she asked if I wear my skirt hemline below or above my knee, and if my cleavage was too low. I assured her that I did not look like a fallen woman, but that I looked pretty much like any other businesswoman. I think it all came together when she realized that we both shop at the same store, Chico's. That's a store I previously swore I would never shop in because it's an "old lady" store. But now, as that brand has become younger and more relevant to younger women and I became older, the conversation evolved to regale in the latest fashions conveyed in the store's most recent catalog.

Nevertheless, this conveyance about me permanently set back my relationship with my mother for the rest of her life, as well as with her husband, who was a childhood neighbor of our family.

Apart from that problematic incident, what was terrifying for me turned out to be more affirming than I had thought. My childhood friends not only accepted me but most of them embraced the "new" me. But most 'moms' reacted differently. One in particular named Joyce—after not having seen me since childhood—and indeed not as my new "self," said at the post-funeral dinner, "Carla, we raised all of you [kids] to be what we wanted you to be, but you all grew up and became who you are." That pretty well summed up the warmth, acceptance, and love of most of my childhood family friends. Unfortunately, most of my transgender friends have been less lucky with family and friends and have faced hostility and estrangement.

Sadly, since I first drafted this book, my mother has passed away, peacefully in her sleep, in a Florida hospice at the age of 90.

To rub salt in the wound for me, in attending her funeral with my six siblings, the night before the funeral, a blended-family dinner was scheduled at an upscale resort. As I was getting dressed a couple of hours before the dinner, I received word through two sisters that my mother's husband (who had never seen me as myself) did not want me to attend the family soirée, and they felt it was best that I did not participate.

That hit me extremely hard. So, I stayed in my motel to the solace of a tuna sandwich. There, I completely fell apart with extreme grief and sadness, having never felt more alone and isolated in my life. I was being cut out of my family meal gathering, the night before my mother's funeral, at a time like no other, when one would want to be with one's family. I sat there thinking about my mother, trying to focus on the happy times I had with her. This was in great contrast to the intense and excruciating pain I was experiencing through the core of my entire being. At that time, I thought of a quote from the Greek poet Aeschylus who said, "There is no pain so great as the memory of joy in present grief," which seemed to help get me through the evening.

As I sat there in my small room, thinking about the death of my mother and confronted with rejection by my family, it brought back terrible dark, repressed memories of the depression, pain, and suicidal ideation I had suffered when I was much younger. To try to alleviate my pain, I walked down by the nearby ocean with these horrifying thoughts swirling in my head, fighting back the tears—wondering how I could even go on.

While walking along the beach, I had decided not to go to the funeral the next day. When I returned to my room, I don't think I ever felt more alone in my life than that night. I then called my brother Tom who had returned from the dinner. Only due to the positive reinforcement and moral support he gave me over a calming glass of wine or two (OK, three), coupled with the incredibly astronomical cost of flying out of a luxury community at the height of tourist season, I was not able to fly home anyway.

My funeral dress.

After struggling all night with the decision to attend or not attend the funeral, as the sun rose over the ocean the next morning, it gave me a renewed sense of hope. I decided at the last minute to go to the funeral out of respect for my mother, realizing that I would get only one shot at honoring her.

So, I went. I had concluded that I did not want to let other people's marginalizing judgment of me, prevent me from honoring the life of my mother for a "crime" I had not committed.

And to add some extra salt to the wound, that morning, as I was getting dressed, one sister suggested that I perhaps should be a "little less girly." That I should run out and quickly buy a pair of pants at the local Walmart. Pants? I don't wear pants. (Maybe I should have told my sister not to look too girly either!)

But if I'm going to continue to live my life as myself, this was not the time to back down to any such ridiculousness. So, I went to the funeral in my black Lauren dress with red flowers that I had planned to wear, and it all went very well.

And I should add that my sister said later that she had been entirely out of line to say what she said to me, apologized, and said I looked exquisite. I guess girls can be girls, particularly in the emotionally charged time of a parent's funeral.

And at the funeral, I particularly enjoyed meeting all the many (senior) friends of my mother in the receiving line, who expressed their condolences, and ironically, told me how proud my mother was of all her children.

Well, unless it was more along the lines of LGBTQ pride, I'm not sure how proud she would have been of me, but who knows. She's now probably looking down on me, making sure my hemline is below my knee. (Thanks, Mom!)

20. Don't Ask

"The most radical thing that any of us can do is to stop projecting our beliefs about gender onto other people's behaviors and bodies."
—Julia Serano PhD, author, performer

Becoming the gender you know you are is one of the most personal, important, and difficult decisions a person can make. Thus, asking that person intrusive questions makes it more difficult, and is as invasive and humiliating as it is rude. Regardless, people have asked me many questions about being transgender. I am extremely open and comfortable answering most any question—particularly from friends—understanding that many people have limited experience with transgender people and are often naturally curious.

However, some questions are simply inappropriate, regardless of whether or not they are about transgender people. For example, here are some questions I've actually been asked and how I feel about them:

1. You look so "real"!

While this is likely said with good intentions, at the same time, it's an undermining and marginalizing statement, since I don't need others to affirm my gender, or subtly imply that this is any way not "real," or that I am trying in any way to mislead someone.

2. I have a friend who is transgender, I've seen one on TV and I know all about it.

It's always good to hear that the person is not completely oblivious to trans people. However, everyone's experience is different and each ought to be respected due to potentially vast differences.

3. So, what's it really like to be transgender?

I was at a restaurant bar I frequent, and the person I was with belted out this question in earshot of the entire establishment. It's not appropriate to "out" a trans person or anyone for that matter—gay, disabled, old, young, black, or any "condition"—with any inappropriate comment without his or her permission. It's a matter of respect, dignity, and privacy. So discretion and valor are the way to go here.

4. You'll always be a male to me, no matter what, so I'll just call you by your former name.

Women have been taking their husbands' surnames for centuries, and generations of humans have had little problem making the switch along with them. For transgender people, like anyone else, it's common decency to be referred to by the names and pronouns they prefer; as often this is their legal name. It's not that difficult to be respectful of this simple, yet most basic, sense of identity people have.

I still get that from a handful of family members. Although it's extremely jarring to be called a name you have not had for a very long time. At the same time, I know this can be very difficult for some, and being comfortable with who I am, and certainly know my legal name, I tend to let it slide, hoping time will help ameliorate this.

5. How do you have sex?

Yes. I've been asked this. I would ask then, "How do you have sex?" Would a casual friend ask that of another person? In polite settings? Anywhere? Is it any of their business? Don't assume that I or any other transgender person wants to be asked about my sex life, any more than anyone else does.

6. Do people assault and rob you because you are transgender?

Unfortunately, I've had the pleasure to have been badly beaten and robbed. Twice. Was it because I am transgender? Cute? Small? Large? Vulnerable? A woman? Was I an easy target? I will never know. Violators are not big on conveying their motives, but does it matter? Does this justify any crime?

Safety is safety for everyone, woman, or man. There are no truly "safe" places to be and one can't live a life of paranoia. However, there are many things everyone can do to increase awareness, know defense tactics, and minimize potentially dangerous situations, regardless of gender.

7. When did you realize you were gay?

Gay? I know this is confounding to some, but it's important to understand that sexuality, gender identity, and anatomical body parts are three very different notions. Trans people can be gay, straight, bisexual, asexual, heterosexual, pansexual, cisgender, gender fluid, or any number of "sexuals." These states can overlap and change over time as well. People like to put people in rigid boxes that don't always exist. However, it's difficult and not appropriate to do so with a gender-variant person (or anyone for that matter) as it is simply not black and white.

8. Did you have "the" surgery?

First of all, there's no one "surgery" trans people have. Like anyone else, they can have many different kinds of surgeries for various ailments and conditions, and trans people can have a variety of transgender-related surgeries as well (if any at all). These are designed to accomplish different results at different times, depending upon what the trans individuals feel, need, or want to do in order to be themselves. Some have surgeries; some don't. Some take hormone therapy; some don't. No matter the medical specifics, gender does not boil down to the presence or absence of reproductive organs. Unless someone volunteers to talk about the subject, transgender people's private parts, like anyone else's, are just that—private.

So what should you ask?

For non-transgender people, the best-case scenario is probably to:

1. Ask them what questions, if any, are appropriate; and

2. Give the trans person an out if he or she feels like you are overstepping your bounds, even though your questions may be born of an innocent curiosity; and

3. Read up on it first, since most transgender information is very accessible today. This makes it a little easier for a trans person to maintain privacy and integrity.

21. Happiness

"Happiness is letting go of what you think your life is supposed to look like by others. Rather, it is celebrating it for everything that it is."
—Mandy Hale

There is nothing wrong with being happy. Loving life. Friends. Things. I will never apologize for my enthusiasm. Once a friend told me I was "exuberant" and ought to seek professional help. Exuberant? Enthusiastic, cheerful, lively, buoyant.

Yes, if one were oscillating between incredible happiness and the depths of depression, yes, from a clinical perspective, this would not be healthy and worthy of psychological exploration. But I am simply happy. At peace.

Recently, the group facilitator, Robert, of what is called a Chalice Circle in my church, shared a wonderful word with me: *eudaimonia*. It's a Greek word commonly translated as happiness, or human flourishing, referring to a state of having a good, in-dwelling spirit or being in a contented state of health, happiness, and encouraging one to live deeply. I believe that is me.

I learned from a person who means a great deal to me not to rely on others for my happiness. I believe that happiness is generated internally and driven spiritually. Of course, I have many great, loving, and supportive friends and family, and I cherish these many wonderful relationships. But my personal happiness is innate. As I shared above, I have firm beliefs rooted in these interrelated five notions, much like a five-sided rose, developed over a lifetime of searching and ultimately finding peace, joy, happiness, spiritual fulfillment, and love.

The beauty of the rose has always moved me and I am connected to the harmony, balance, dignity, and divine grace represented in its five petals, shape, and colors. The rose is an enduring symbol of radiating joy and completeness. Although they always have five sides, roses vary in size and shape, and display in rainbow colors, ranging from white through yellows and reds, blues, and pinks (male and female)? The rose represents beauty and growth, love and compassion. Flowers speak to our inner soul in a way that's difficult to explain. And of course, if one tries to defile a rose, you will get pricked! Five also enumerates the many states of being in other cultures.

I don't think about the idea of five all the time, only in my "MEPPS" idea, where it's certainly prevalent in my life. More importantly, I think as I grow older, I find that true inner happiness does not come from material things, but rather, it's more about being surrounded by nature and a spiritual presence; to have old friends, new friends, and family with whom you chat, laugh, talk, play music, talk about north-south-east-west, heaven, and earth. And of course, knowing and being who you are, your authentic and innate self. That is true happiness to me.

22. *My Beautiful Daughters*

I have two daughters. Two wonderful daughters. I love them both very much and believe they love me, too. They provide me extraordinary joy and happiness. I am incredibly proud of them. They also accept me for who I am, as a loving, caring, if not somewhat doting parent, like I suppose every parent is. I am most grateful for that.

I wish everyone were as enlightened, loving, and caring as my own two daughters. They are a significant source of my deep and innate sense of joy and happiness. I love it when people look me deep in the eyes and whisper the question, "Do your daughters accept you?" Yes. They do. They always have. When I told them a long time ago about me, each resounded back to me with, "Yes, I know." They both had always seen me more as feminine persona than a male one.

23. *I've Gotta Be Me*

As I finish writing this book, the popular song, *I've Gotta Be Me,* which first appeared in the short-lived 1969 Broadway musical *Golden Rainbow* came up on the radio, sung by Sammy Davis Jr. I didn't know when I first heard it years ago or how much it was a foreshadowing of my life.

Perhaps because it seemed somewhat "schmaltzy" at the time, I had never really connected with it, at least not conscientiously. But hearing it again after a long hiatus, I was moved to tears (I guess that's part of being a woman). I paused and actually listened to the lyrics closely for the first time. Every word resonated.

In essence, the song expresses the idea that you can't live to be right for somebody else. You can only be what and who you are. To not give up on your dream of life since that is what keeps you alive. *I've Gotta Be Me* is also a documentary film examining Sammy Davis, Jr.'s journey for identity through his complex, complicated, and contradictory life, within the backdrop of American bigotry. Davis spent his whole life confronting obstacles. He was also Puerto Rican, reportedly bisexual, and the most public black figure to embrace Judaism, thus yoking his identity to another persecuted minority.

24. Going Forward

Society often lags behind science. I've lived a life as a woman for most of my life. I am like any other woman. I have the same concerns, challenges, fears, fun, joys, and freedom that any woman lives with or pursues. In fact, I forget that I was ever anything else. As you've read, I spent the earlier part of my life trying to conceal who I really was. It's odd to think—how decades ago – I had to hide who I really was inside.

Now, I have the opposite problem—I sometimes have to hide that I was ever anyone else than who I am today, particularly with potential clients or work prospects. This is due to antiquated and ill-informed societal "norms," stemming from a lack of knowledge, understanding, and acceptance of information that is readily available in any medical journal or a quick perusal through Wikipedia.

We need to eliminate the artificial boxes that attempt to create categories for the highly complex world of gender, sex, and body type, and identify the barriers to transgender knowledge, understanding, and equality. We need to have informed, intelligent discussions about how to create a message that removes these barriers through accuracy, timeliness, and comprehensiveness. Doing so can raise the bar of what we're capable of accomplishing as a society when we move out of the compendium of misinformation.

Today, with the support systems I have in place, friends, most of my family, the confidence I have in who I am, and the willingness to put myself out there and be a voice for not only myself, but for many others like me—together provide great solace and confidence in knowing I can be myself. Even those who are not transgender and are struggling with other or related issues have reached out to me and thanked me for staying true to myself and being a positive voice in an often-discriminatory world.

25. Respect

Comedian Rodney Dangerfield built his incredibly memorable brand with, "I don't get no respect." That is the challenge I, as a transgender person, face almost daily. I think the most important thing is to be aware that gender-variant people exist everywhere but aren't all the same. However, if we have anything in common, I think we all would simply ask for respect—no different than anyone else—respect for those who deviate from traditionally perceived male or female traits and characteristics. If you have a belief system and your belief system is shattered, you have no framework.

I've learned that the main thing in life is understanding and accepting who you are. To be your authentic self. Otherwise, you will never attain true happiness. I've learned over time to understand that if people don't accept you, I now ask, "Who cares?" I find that as a result, I have better friends in my life. I know them to be caring, supportive, and loving.

I am not a woman who is going to hurt your kids in public bathrooms, nor do I need to be prayed for or fixed. I am not broken. I just seek love, compassion, and kindness. No one should ever have to suffer because of who he or she is or appears or identifies to be. The more education that's out there about what it means to be different, the better. If society denies our identities and our experiences, intentionally "mis-genders" us, or refers to us by former names, it only makes our already challenging lives even more difficult.

Some 43 percent of trans people attempt suicide at some point in their lives, and many succeed. When we're surrounded by allies, when we're respected for who we are, when we're able to live in a world in which diversity is celebrated and all people are respected, valued, and affirmed, inclusive of their gender identity and gender expression, we will see that number decline.

Do people not realize the terrible hurt felt inside when we're marginalized and misaligned for something we have no control of, let alone fully understand? Is it really so much to ask—to be treated like everyone else, to have the same rights as everyone else? That's really all anyone would ever ask for.

If you have a transgender person in your life, unless asked, it's best not to subject the person to personal and invasive questions about their transition, particularly the medical aspects of their transition. Most of all, if you wish to be a friend of someone you know who is LGBTQ, I say, just be kind and supportive.

26. *What I Want*

*"This is reality for us, and all we ask for is acceptance
and validation for what we say that we are.
It's as basic as that."*
—Andreja Pejic

I want the same things that most people want. I want to be a good parent to my children, contribute to society, make a difference, be a good friend, have good friends, and be close to my family—at least those who can accept me for who I am, rather than who they were once led to believe I was.

What I hope for is a day where there is no distinction between who's gay, who's straight, who's trans, who's not. What does it matter?

I simply want to be treated like a human being. With dignity and respect, with valid feelings and the human rights anyone else would expect. I would want that people realize that those expressing a gender different from the one they were assigned at birth are often undergoing and struggling with a major life-changing event. Patience, understanding, and a willingness to discuss issues these changes bring about would help them through a potentially difficult and emotional time.

As difficult as it is for a person who isn't a member of the transgender community to do so, I ask that others try to under-stand the courage it takes to be true to oneself—especially when that self doesn't match the anatomy assigned at birth. Know that those coming out are often doing so with great trepidation and fear, realizing that while pockets of tolerance are expanding, discriminatory policies and hostile, uninformed attitudes remain widespread.

Although the tide is slowly shifting, unfortunately lives, careers, and dreams hang in the balance. People deserve to come out in a world where stories of compassion and support vastly outnumber those that end with a suicide note.

I don't want "special treatment." I just want to be respected as a human being, a friend, a parent, a sister, a cousin, a daughter, and as a professional—deserving the same dignity, worthiness, and respect as anyone else.

I want to be judged by merit and substance. By action and character. I want to be able to exist in the world without the core of my identity being dismissed by someone who couldn't possibly understand what it's like, no matter how many times they've "been around the world."

I don't want to be marginalized by someone who is judgmental, dismissive, condescending, critical, condemnatory, trivializing, arrogant, and all-knowing about what a transgender person is all about, while not having been one themselves.

I ask that people:

- Not assume they know what a trans person's experience is. There are many ways in which differences in gender identity are expressed. The idea of being "trapped in a man/woman's body," the belief that trans women are hyper-feminine, or trans men are hyper-masculine, or the belief that all trans people will seek hormones and surgery, are all stereotypes that apply to some but not others.

- Not impose theories they may have learned third-hand, or assume that the experience of other trans people they may know is the same as that of the person in front of them.

- Not assume that one is "transitioning" because of a past trauma in his or her life, or that the individual is changing genders as a way to escape from their bodies or other aspects of their life.

- Be direct, open, and honest. Realize this is often extremely difficult for transgender people as well, and try to understand what they may have gone through or are going through to become their true and authentic self.

- Be willing to listen, learn, and try to understand and accept someone different than themselves.

I want the world to see me for me, and to be able to live a normal life without fear of being brutalized or mugged, or being accused of having some sort of "perverted" or malicious intentions.

And finally, I ask that people not obfuscate or gossip. If someone is finding something difficult, let the trans person know. Directly. An honest, straightforward response is a lot easier for someone to deal with than cutting off all communications. We're all human beings searching for meaning in our lives. Like anyone else, I want to be able to live and work, love and be loved by friends and family without worrying about being judged, bullied, harassed, injured, or even killed for who I am.

27. The Road—Taken

I've always been an exceedingly joyful person. The only professional help I've ever needed (and received) was to help process why a few people have hated me due to their perception of who they thought I was or wanted me to be, preventing me from living in a world that would allow me to be myself. Such a vitriolic sense of hatred was usually due to a lack of information, understanding, and acceptance.

Being transgender is a mental, emotional, physical, medical, and psychological phenomenon. It can also cause a myriad of medical issues, such as depression, anxiety, suicidal ideation, and possibly death. This can happen when you try to suppress your authentic self. Without professional help and/or treatment, a large network of supportive friends, colleagues, and most of my family members, I, too, would most likely be dead today.

Socrates, choosing death instead of exile from Athens or holding his tongue in silence, observed famously that "an unexamined life is not worth living." Now, when I look into a mirror, my life simply seems normal. In that spirit, I cannot be anyone other than who I am.

The female in me is who I am. It is how I present myself and live. I've known who I am and what I was since the cradle. I now have a sense of inner peace and happiness. Freed. Comfortable. Happy. That is an incredible, and I might say, a rare feeling to have. To get up in the morning. Get dressed. Go to work. And just be a normal woman.

I once was a male. I once was a transgender woman. Today I am simply a woman. I am in every way one can be. I've been accepted that way by friends and colleagues, new and old, and by most of my family.

Recently, a friend said to me, "Carla, you seem so happy." I said I was. But this is about life. My life. About who I really am. I cherish it and would never want to end it prematurely. But it took two marriages, two divorces, and one gender change to become that way, and yes, I am happy.

Although this is the end of a very long road toward gaining respect, obtaining dignity, and becoming me, now it's about going forward and beginning a new chapter and pursuing many renewed and new life dreams and passions. I am a woman, and this is what it's like.

However, there are some downsides to becoming a woman. I've had to come to terms with the fact that I'll have to live a life without pockets—perhaps this less-traveled road is the one I've taken, but for me that's made all the difference for the better—a life I can live as my true self.

Epilogue

Touched by an Angel

I did not know Carla Anne Ernst until I received a phone call from her several months ago. She informed me that she knew my daughter Karis Anne Ross through her circle of friends called "Girls Night Out," who had regularly convened for dinner in a safe and fun place to socialize, and to be a support system for each other.

Carla told me of this book, *Life Without Pockets*, and asked for my permission to dedicate it to my daughter. I was touched, and of course said yes. After our first call, it was as if I had known Carla all of our lives. In fact, I am grateful Carla contacted me.

My daughter took her life at the end of 2014. Her light had gone out. Her suicide letter conveyed that she could no longer live with being bullied by people—especially the staff in the school where she had worked. The bullying had gone on for more than 10 years. Her ultimate suicide was an unspeakably tragic and horrific event, especially since years earlier, Karis was elated with her transformation, and finally felt free to live authentically. But life's challenges as a transgender woman and her strong emotions, including deeply hidden depression, got the best of her.

Carla expressed to me how much she and everyone loved my daughter, and how moved she was by the abundant friends and family with their words and performances at Karis' Life Celebration.

Carla has graciously dedicated this book to Karis for many reasons, one being the goal of the book—to end suicide among the transgender community. Karis would have been so proud of her for writing the book and stepping up to the plate in telling her own personal story, as I am. I know all too well about the struggles and challenges transgender individuals face, but Carla has surpassed them and is going forward with her message.

When I wrote about Karis in an inspirational book about joy, I said, "Even in the face of controversy, Karis remained a true trailblazer, determined to align with who she really was, beyond the external definitions of gender and appearance." I know that Karis lives on in the clouds (I call them "Karis Clouds"), smiling down on us, touching our hearts every day, knowing we are carrying her mantle forward.

Like my own daughter, Carla is a trailblazer, an advocate, a friend, a mentor, and a hero. A strong and dedicated woman. *Life Without Pockets* is a step towards humanizing what these wonderful souls courageously go through each and every day of their lives. Let us see people as whole people. As human beings. I see Carla, like my own daughter, and so many others, as someone who is living out an authentic life. No labels. No marginalization. No hate.

I see my new friend Carla Anne Ernst as being a woman— which clearly she is—and of course, living a life with NO pockets! Thank you, Carla for writing your story, and for dedicating your book to our beloved angel, Karis.

—Jill E. Greinke, mother of Karis Anne Ross

Acknowledgments

It's difficult to acknowledge each and every one of my wonderful friends, family, extended family, neighbors, and colleagues—all of whom have been able to accept and respect me as a human being, beyond my gender identity. These people endure as life-long stalwarts, and most importantly, have helped me in so many ways to get this story told. I don't know how I would have survived without their love, friendship, and support—or ever finished this book!

I have many dear life-long friends, but for starters, Clay Frohman and Chip Mack, who have always been an integral part of shaping my life. Another person, my longtime music partner, gifted singer, songwriter, and composer extraordinaire, Roye Anastasio, with whom I have written music for broadcast TV, radio, and film, and who has always been there for me on many levels. Nothing is more exhilarating than staying up all night, boosting bass tracks, and battling over mixing a masterful music track with Roye!

Others whom I've always been particularly close to since my earliest days and who have helped me to get this book written in one way or another, are my siblings Barbara Anne Kolich, Susan Marie Corser, Sally Williams, Tom Ernst, Elizabeth Nugent; extended family – my Aunt Mary Ernst, cousins Nancy Anderson, Jim Ernst, Bob Ernst, Paul Ernst, Karen Henricks, Gretchen Catherwood, Laura Ernst, Kathy Geertz-Schopp—and my unofficial research director and family genealogist, John Geertz-Larson. And of course, my amazing daughters, Sarah Marie Ernst and Margaret Anne Ernst, whose unconditional love and support have given me a reason to go on.

Life-long childhood friends include parasitologist and zoologist Frank Sherwin and sister / journalist Elizabeth Sherwin, and blues radio host Corey Niebank. Exceptional musicians and composers, Marcy Smalley in Kansas City, Becky Keen, Steve Samler, and Jerry Zervic in Chicago, Eric Bikales in Nashville, and the extraordinary jazz performer and writer, Fred Haas, at Dartmouth College. Hollywood film editor Barbara Kaplan and her family, head "idea guy," author, TEdX speaker, Bryan Mattimore. Communications sage and mentor Geoffrey Pickard. Yoga instructor, researcher on Brazilian popular culture, and talented photographer Meredith Watts (cover photo of this book). Writers and authors Trish Hundhausen, Barbara Shapiro, Linda Yellin, and Scott Johnson; and the Reverends Dena McPhetres, Jennifer Nordstrom, Robert Ater, and Jean Dow. Lovely life friends, Lindsey Lang, Anne Curley, and Peter and Jill Lundgren.

My healthcare providers, Kathy Hernandez, MD, and counselor Melissa Waldo, LCSW at the 16th Street Clinic. My childhood pediatrician, Dr. Bennet R. Sherman (deceased), audiologist and book club fan, Marcia Dewey, AuD, John Gielow, PSY.D. Fact checkers at the Glencoe Public Library and Glencoe Historical Society; and sanity-checkers, moral support-ers, and amazing friends Anne Clements, Linda Grace, Julie

Hart, Georgia Henry, Pat Parcell, Al Jaberg, Amy Wilbourne, John Ryan, Renee Silverman, and Don Warshaw.

This book would not have been complete without the thoughtful and kind words of advertising research guru and life-long friend Peter Switzer; and friend, counselor, and gifted writer, Jill Grienke—writers of the *Foreword* and *Epilogue*, respectively, bookending the work.

Of course, this book could not have been written, nor the story been told, without my book editor and publisher extraordinaire, HenschelHAUS Publishing founder, President/CEO and book maven, Kira Henschel. With the patience of Job, she has provided constant guidance, direction, insight, support, billions of typo fixes, encouragement, and merriment—without which this book would not exist. When I first met her, she said when she first saw the manuscript, "This story needs to be told." Also, thanks to our mutual friend, Emmy award-winning video producer Mark Concannon, who connected me with Kira in the first place.

Thank you also to the medical and transgender community— educators, artists, writers, photographers, and authors willing to share information with me to help assure accuracy for this book.

And to my lifelong friend, Janet Downing, who is my mental, emotional, spiritual, and social compass, healer, advisor, and sage, who's critical and constant review of this work has been the greatest gift I could ever receive.

It is impossible to acknowledge everyone who contributed to this book, as almost daily a comment was conveyed or reference made providing more insight that helped provide elucidation to the complex topic of gender identity. Thus, I apologize to others whom I may have overlooked, those who have asked questions, have provided comments and feedback when they read drafts of chapters—all of whom I'm sure I will remember as soon as the book is printed (I guess that's what second printings are for).

About the Author

Selfie by Carla Ernst
(Annie Leibovitz was booked)

Carla Anne Ernst currently lives in Milwaukee, Wisconsin, where she is active as an author and corporate communications writer, and volunteers in several groups such as Deaf Unity in Madison, Common Ground Southeastern Wisconsin, and the Salvation Army of Chicago. Carla has served in senior-level communications positions for GE Healthcare and Johnson & Johnson, and at top-tier public relations firms Hill & Knowlton and Burson-Marsteller in New York. She has produced award-winning films for PBS and A&E such as *To Dance for Gold, First Born,* and *Fifty Years to Mackinac.* Carla's also a performing woodwind instrumentalist (clarinet, flute and saxophone) and ASCAP film composer, and loves going to classical and jazz concerts, theater, ballet, museums, and off-the-beaten-path art exhibits.

Carla was included as a subject in the 2016 Photo Exhibition *Our Trans Family,* (http://www.mkelgbt.org/trans-family-project/) photographs of transgender people and their families in Wisconsin. The Exhibition is designed to foster greater understanding about people who identify as transgender, the broad range of people who identify as "gender fluid," and those who do not identify with a binary definition of their gender.

For fun, Carla enjoys going "UpNort" to her family summer lake cottage in Wild Rose, Wisconsin, where she likes to race sailboats, canoe, kayak, eat sweet corn and brats, and have a Point beer (or two...OK, three), and where she plays clarinet in the Waupaca City Band.

She's not old, but also not new. She grew up in the age of electricity. In her day, when you turned off a light switch, it never asked, "Are you sure you want to turn it off?" It never crashed, had memory issues, had to be re-booted or said, "You've created a fatal error." Fatal? Seems a bit extreme. It's a brave new world.

Carla can be contacted at:

Carla@lifewithoutpockets.info

www.lifewithoutpockets.info

(414) 614-6873